SIMPLY
GIVE THANKS

A Beginner's Guide to Joyful Living through the Power of Spiritual Gratitude

Change your Thoughts & Actions to Become a New You!

MELISSA ALVAREZ

Adrema Press

Copyright © 2013 by Melissa Alvarez
Author Websites: www.MelissaAlvarez.com and www.APsychicHaven.com

ISBN: 978-1-59611-112-7

Cover and Book Design by Melissa Alvarez at BookCovers.Us
Cover Art Background © DepositPhotos.com / David Schrader / Bas Meelker

All Rights Reserved. No part of this book may be reproduced by any method whatsoever. Except for use in any review, the reproduction or utilization of this work in whole or in part in any form by any electronic, mechanical or other means, now known or hereafter invented, including xerography, photocopying and recording, or in any information or retrieval system, is forbidden without the prior written permission of both the publisher and copyright owner of this book.

First Trade Paperback Printing: July 2013
10 9 8 7 6 5 4 3 2 1

> If you purchased this book without a cover, you should be aware that this book is stolen property. It was reposted as "unsold and destroyed" to the publisher, and neither the author nor the publisher has received any payment for this "stripped book."

Other books by Melissa Alvarez

365 Ways to Raise Your Frequency
The 365 Days to Raise Your Frequency Journal
Your Psychic Self
Simply Give Thanks
Simply Give Thanks Gratitude Journal
Analyze Your Handwriting
Your Color Power
Ghosts, A Spirit Guide and A Past Life
Chakra Divination® Cards & Charts Activity Book
The Essential Guide To Chakra Divination
Chakra Divination Ultimate Balance Journal
The eLink Directory of Paranormal Investigative Groups Around the World
Homemade Recipes for Horse Treats plus Fly Sprays & Tips for Owners
The Phoenix's Guide To Self Renewal
Christmas Desserts
Penelope Panda's Shooting Star

Writing as Ariana Dupré
Paranormal Romantic Suspense

Night Visions
Paradise Designs
Briar Mountain
Talgorian Dragon
Talgorian Prophecy

Websites:
MelissaA.com
BookCoversGalore.com
BookCovers.Us
APsychicHaven.com

"As we express our gratitude,
we must never forget that the highest
appreciation is not to utter words,
but to live by them."
-John Fitzgerald Kennedy

——Dedication——

To my wonderful parents, Warren and Nancy McDowell, for teaching me grateful appreciation during the toughest of times, how to look for silver linings in the clouds, and implementing the classic philosophy "the shortest distance between two points is a straight line" will always make life more efficient. I love you both to the extreme!

Acknowledgements

On every journey there are those that help us along the way. That certainly is the case in the creation of this book. I offer my sincerest gratitude to those who have supported my efforts as a writer.

First and foremost I thank my family for their support during the writing process. For understanding when I don't answer them right away it's usually because I'm so deep in thought I didn't even hear them. As a writer working in the middle of many potential distractions, I've learned to focus within and tune out the background noise—sometimes too much.

My gratitude also goes to each and every one of you who chose to read *365 Ways to Raise Your Frequency, Your Psychic Self* and my other fiction and nonfiction titles. Thank you from the bottom of my heart for deciding to spend some time with me by reading my books.

Smiles,

Melissa

——Disclaimer——

1) The author is not a doctor and does not give medical advice. If you are experiencing a medical condition such as anxiety, depression or mental illness then you should seek professional medical attention and consult with a doctor to determine the best course of treatment for your condition.

2) The examples shared with you in this book are the author's personal experiences. Your experiences may be similar to or completely different from the author's examples. The way the author experiences spiritual gratitude, is based on her personal beliefs and interpretations, just as your experiences are based upon your personal beliefs and interpretations of spirituality. This book is intended to be a guide to being more spiritual grateful, not the final word on the subject.

Contents

Introduction 1

One: The Practice of Spiritual Gratitude 07
 Begin With Yourself 08
  Exercise: Begin Within 11
 Defining Spiritual Gratitude 12
 Create a New You by Awakening to Spiritual Gratitude 16
 Shifting from Ingratitude to Spiritual Gratitude 19
 Spiritual Gratitude and Unhappiness Can't Co-exist 23
 Daily Practice Is Important 27

Two: Spiritual Gratitude and Soul Purpose 31
 Be Authentic and True to Your Soul's Purpose 32
  Exercise: Find Your Soul Purpose 33
 It's Not About Money or Material Things 35
 Don't Let Ingratitude Destroy Your Soul Purpose 38
 Do and Be What You Believe 41
 Be Spiritually Grateful for Your Own Path 44

Three: Spiritual Gratitude and The Spirit Connection 49
 Seek Out the Sacred 49
 Become Whole through Spiritual Gratitude 52
 The Transformative Power of Spiritual Gratitude 56
  Exercise: Connect to Spiritual Gratitude 57

Exercise: A Conversation with Spiritual Gratitude   59

Connecting to Spirit   62

   Exercise: Connect to Your Spirit   64

Recognize the Support You Receive   66

Four: Spiritual Gratitude in Action   69

Remember to Act with Spiritual Gratitude   69

Take Time to Share   73

Forgiveness and Spiritual Gratitude   76

   Exercise: Forgiveness   77

Forgiving Yourself   78

Fill Your Expectations with Spiritual Gratitude   80

Embrace Life, Live with Intent from the Soul   83

   Exercise: Take Stock of Your Intentions   85

Create a Journal, Make a List, Board or Chart   87

Five: Slow It Down to Simplify Your Life   91

Be Spiritually Grateful for the Small Things   92

   Exercise: Finding the Little Things   94

Let Go of What No Longer Belongs in Your Life   95

Only What You Need   99

Follow Your Dreams   102

Live in Love and Spiritual Gratitude   105

Six: Change Your Attitude to Open Your Heart   109

Sense of Entitlement   109

Release Resentment   113

Exercise: Shed Negative Feelings   116
No One Knows Everything   117
Don't Compare Yourself with Anyone Else   120
Turn Past Hurts into Gifts through Spiritual Gratitude   123
Become Worry and Stress Free   126
People Are Drawn to Your Spiritual Gratuitous Light   129

Seven: Spiritual Gratitude During Difficult Times   133
Transitions, Changes and Spiritual Gratitude   133
Spiritual Gratitude during Illness, Sadness, and Loss   137
    Exercise: Find the Positive   143
Choosing to Move Forward   144
Reconnect with the Flow of Life   147

Eight: Grace, Wisdom & Spiritual Gratitude   151
Hidden Blessings   151
Spiritual Substance and Gratitude   154
Look At Life from a Universal Perspective   157
Spiritual Gratitude Gives Second Chances   160
Heal Your Soul   163
The Miracle that You Are   167
    Exercise: The Uniqueness in You   168

Nine: Practice Joyful Living Every Day   171
Building Gratefulness in You and Thankfulness in Others   171
Participate In the Arts to Stimulate Spiritual Gratitude   174
Be of Service to Others   178

Give Back through Random Acts of Kindness   181
    Exercise: Random Acts of Kindness   184
Discover and Follow Your Divine Path   184

Ten: How to Activate Thankfulness Now   189
Ready, Set, Activate!   189
Experience Spiritual Gratitude in the Now   192
    Exercise: Living in the Moment   192
Teach Others to Be Spiritually Grateful   195
Remain Spiritually Grateful at the Core of Your Soul   197

Bibliography   201

—— Introduction ——

Thanks for choosing to spend some time with me today within the pages of this book. I decided to write about spiritual gratitude after experiencing difficult circumstances in my life when it was hard for me to feel thankful for anything at all. During those times, it seemed as if my world had just crumbled at my feet. When things went bad, they went really bad. I would become overly stressed, I worried about every little thing and I forgot to look at the positive influences around me or to be thankful for the good things in my life. When I realized my energy was off balance I purposefully made changes to bring myself back to center. I made a conscious effort to appreciate the little things in my life that were going well. Things that I normally wouldn't think about but when I became aware, I could appreciate them. The result was that I became more grateful deep within my spirit. Once I realized the power in the results of being spiritually grateful, then even if things weren't going well, they didn't appear so overwhelmingly devastating. Now I do my best to remain spiritually grateful every day.

I noticed the same thing happening to other people who were going through hard times. When they purposefully shifted their energy and way of thinking to one of spiritual gratitude, it brought about significant change. It is my intention, within these pages, to help you learn to focus on the positive by simply giving thanks through spiritual gratitude. It's easy to forget to be thankful when you lead a busy life but spiritual gratitude is a gift you can give to yourself. When you become aware and awakened to your essential spiritual self, you'll find an appreciation of life that will lead to more joyful living.

The purpose of this book is to help you make spiritual gratitude a regular practice in your daily life to aid in positive growth and self-improvement, which will help you experience more happiness and joy.

Spiritual gratitude is about changing your thought patterns in order to change your actions which will change your life.

This book is designed to empower you to create tremendous positivity in your life by becoming more spiritually grateful. This isn't a religious book. When I discuss *spirit* I'm talking about the spirit within you, the spirits that watch over you and the spirit in which you live your life. This book is about feeling spiritual gratitude while recognizing your soul essence and through the connection you make to the Divine and Universal Consciousness. It is written as a beginner's guide; with exercises throughout the chapters that will show and teach you how to enhance your life through spiritual gratitude. It is meant to be a resource you can turn to time and time again, especially when you feel ungrateful or when life is off-kilter. It is my hope that this book will help guide you back on track during times of unbalance and that my words can enlighten you and bring you the focus needed to be spiritually grateful every day of your life.

You might say to me, "How can I be thankful, Melissa? My life is in shambles!" If this describes your way of thinking at this very moment, then today is the perfect day to start living in spiritual gratitude. I've worn those same shoes and when you have nothing else to lose, you *can* begin to move forward again by appreciating what you have left, even if that's *only* yourself. Life is hard. The only constant within it is change. It is demanding and you'll face challenges each and every day, whether they're small, large or life-altering. Life can be a frustrating battle at times, but that doesn't mean that you can't rise above the problems, if only for a moment, to appreciate the positive in your life.

We've all been in the trenches at some point. We've had our worlds torn apart by some financial disaster, by people treating us poorly, or we've felt as if everything that could possibly go wrong went wrong. By practicing spiritual gratitude on a daily basis, you will soon be able to see problems in a different light and be thankful for the lessons learned from any bad experiences. With this change, you can become a beacon of light not only within yourself, but to those around you. Positive changes will come your way and it all starts by being spiritually aware and grateful.

I'm not going to kid you. Depending on your situation, learning to be spiritually grateful can be hard to accomplish. Some life experiences are extremely difficult and you may be in the midst of one of them right now. Being spiritually grateful isn't always as easy as just thinking happy thoughts or picking the positive. Sure, *sometimes* it can be that easy, but often it requires you to understand yourself and your choices at a soul level; and to actively choose and be consciously aware that you *are* choosing spiritual gratitude over some other emotion. It is feeling grateful within your core spiritual being instead of simply giving lip service to the words *thank you* or *I'm grateful for*....

In this book I'm not going to address anything of a medical nature. If you're dealing with mental illness, anxiety, depression or any other medical situation, then you need to contact a medical professional to help you with those issues. I am not a doctor and it is not my place to discuss medical issues.

As you're learning to be spiritually grateful, remember the opposite of spiritual gratitude is ungratefulness. The negativity of ungratefulness can't co-exist with the powerful positivity of being spiritually grateful. There will be days when you'll feel sad, when you'll feel angry, hurt, or simply ungrateful—that's human nature. It's normal to have these types of feelings because you *are* human. It's how human beings function. Sometimes you have to experience the bad to appreciate the good. And some things in life are just plain hard to deal with. But you also have the ability to choose to make changes in your life. You can wallow in despair, or, after experiencing sadness, you can consciously pick yourselves up and move forward in life. It's all about making choices and the choice is yours to make.

Spiritual gratitude, spirituality and consciousness are all connected to the cosmos of divine knowledge, all of which identify you as a spiritual being at your purest essence.

Spiritual gratitude is filled with transformative energy. The simple act of taking the time to be grateful can turn your life around. It doesn't happen in the blink of an eye but instead you become more aware and in that awareness you will be transformed. Spiritual gratitude will give you a sense of peace. From the peace within comes a greater understanding of the world around you.

As you live your life you're always learning and growing on a spiritual level. You learn from your mistakes, grow on your path of self-discovery and embody all that you are as a spiritual being.

When you let your light shine, accept your true spiritual essence and nature, and are thankful in all of your experiences, then you grow spiritually and become more empowered.

Love, selflessness, joy, caring and compassion are all keys of spiritual gratitude. When you put these keys into the locks of your life, you open yourself to the wonders that the Universe has to offer you on every level. Now is the time to become one with your Divine Self, to open the doors of your mysteries and be thankful every step of the way. You hold these keys in your hands. It's up to you whether you use them to empower your own soul essence or whether you allow them to sit idly by as you delve into negativity. It is your choice to be spiritually grateful and find the joy that you seek if you will only insert these keys into the locks of your life.

For those who have learned to be spiritually grateful, it often becomes a way of life. It is so interwoven into their being that it happens without conscious thought. It is part of who they are, how they behave and how they interact with others. Look at the people in your life. Do you know someone who lives this way? Have you noticed that they often don't experience much negativity? They may have just as many dramatic things happen in their lives as anyone else but they handle it differently because they are looking at the situations with spiritual gratitude. Sure, some may falter, everyone does at some point because we're all human, but they return quickly to their way of thinking and situations seem to resolve smoothly and quickly. It can be the same way for you.

Now is the time to begin. Are you ready? You can do this! Through your gratefulness and actions you can transform your life. The goal is to live in joy, love, and oneness with your spiritual essence. It all begins by simply giving thanks in every aspect of your life. It takes faith in yourself and the path you walk every day. It may call for changes in your way of thinking, in your actions and reactions. It may mean keeping your mouth shut when you want to talk, or to talk when you'd prefer to stay quiet.

Living in spiritual gratitude is recognizing the truth of your soul, living that truth and appreciating yourself and those around you through your daily experiences. It's said that truth can free you. Thankfulness and spiritual gratitude not only frees you to be your true self, but brings joy and happiness too. Embrace your truth and be thankful in spirit.

—1—
The Practice of Spiritual Gratitude

Have you ever paid attention to how much better you feel when you're in a grateful frame of mind? Feeling appreciation often makes you feel more blessed because you're actively attentive to the good things in your life instead of focusing on what is lacking. Both gratefulness and ungratefulness are based on your state of mind and your beliefs. You can choose to be grateful and pay attention to what you are thankful for in life or you can choose ungratefulness by giving attention to the things that are going wrong in your life. It is far better to choose spiritual gratitude because the positive effects can be life changing. Let's begin by defining spiritual gratitude.

Spiritual gratitude: the quality or feeling of being grateful and thankful within your core spiritual being, your soul essence, and allowing the positive energy of thankfulness to flow from your spiritual self out into the Universe, positively affecting the people and world around you.

Spirituality is the belief that your spirit can reach higher levels of consciousness through your connection to God, the Universe, the way you think about life, your connection to nature and through the enlightenment of your internal self on a soul level. Your commitment to growing in spirit is spirituality. When you connect mind, body and spirit you will find harmony and balance in life. You can do this by becoming more aware of yourself, your environment, the people you interact with daily and the simplicities in life. When spiritual gratitude becomes part of your daily practice, you will find you can make a positive impact on others as well.

Spiritual gratitude also enables the body, mind and spirit to heal through the acknowledgement and appreciation of our own personal situations. You are a miracle, a loving, grateful spiritual entity and it is your time to shine.

Begin With Yourself

Whenever you want to change something in your life, the place to start is with yourself. If you plan to use spiritual gratitude to help you heal then look inside to find ways to accept and heal from painful situations in your past and present. You have to begin with yourself in order to share spiritual gratitude with others. Give second chances, be supportive and change negatives to positives to heal your soul.

This is also true of living a life filled with spiritual gratitude. You have to love and appreciate yourself first before you can feel these emotions for other people or expect them to reciprocate in kind. When you put feelings of spiritual gratitude into the world it positively affects those around you. They in turn usually respond in kind to you. When you give spiritual gratitude you receive it back in as well.

If you have negative feelings about yourself as a person or spiritual being, then you have to address these feelings in the beginning. Look at the things that you don't like about yourself and if you desire a change, make it. If there's nothing about yourself that you want to change, but there are some things you dislike, then through spiritual gratitude you can learn to be thankful for your imperfections. When you love yourself, you are naturally thankful for your life and unique talents. You are worthy of positivity in your life simply because you are here. You were born, given life, and you don't have to prove to anyone that you are worthy of loving yourself or of being spiritually grateful. You are worthy because you are you.

Loving yourself has nothing to do with living up to the expectations of another person. Someone else may not like you, may think little of you, think that you haven't accomplished anything in your life or even feel that they are better than you. That is *their* issue, *not* yours. You can't let someone else's opinion affect the love you feel for yourself. Be proud of your accomplishments, be happy with what you're able to do in life, look at what makes you the unique person that you are and love yourself for it. The negative opinions of others can be harmful if you cling to them or embrace them as your own thoughts and feelings.

Sometimes, past hurts or things people said that negatively affected your self-esteem can prevent you from fully loving yourself, especially if you've carried those feelings within you for many years. If you discover something like this within you when you're making spiritual gratitude a part of your daily routine, then face the experience, accept it as what it is—someone else's opinion—and let it go. Don't let another person's negativity keep you from loving yourself.

Work internally to give yourself permission to forgive any past wrongs by others and give yourself permission to forgive any wrongs that you may have committed against someone else.

Making a list is a great way to sort out these types of feelings. If there are things that you feel guilty about, times when you wronged someone else, or that you could have done something to help another person but didn't, then you have to address those situations in your mind and in your heart but first you have to recognize them within yourself. Guilt can hold you back from loving yourself and allowing your life to be filled with spiritual gratitude because guilt makes you feel unworthy. How can you feel thankful if you feel undeserving?

It's important to understand the immense significance of the wondrous spiritual being that you are to have a clear understanding of why you should live in spiritual gratitude on the earthly plane. Releasing guilt and forgiving yourself allows you take responsibility for your life. If you find it difficult to be responsible for your own actions, then step back and reflect on your true purpose.

Each of us is responsible for our every thought, word, and action. If you're not accepting that responsibility then it's time to regroup. It's easy to blame things on someone or something else or to make excuses for your actions instead of admitting you made a conscious choice to do something even if that choice wasn't the smartest one to make. Admitting mistakes is hard to do but to heal it's a step you need to take.

Once you have worked with spiritual gratitude from the inside out, you'll begin to notice that more and more gifts flow from Universal Energy to you. You're able to see them clearly, and because you've taken care of yourself from the inside out, you're more eager to accept them. You've cleared away any old patterns of negative behavior and are embracing positive actions and are no longer restricting yourself by backing yourself into corners or working against your own well-being. Instead, there is forward movement and positive flow within you.

To get to this point, you have to begin. Beginning can be the hardest part because by beginning you're also committing to making things better for yourself. Facing the past hurts and mistakes can be difficult but until you do it, you're not giving spiritual gratitude a chance to help you turn your life around.

Begin today.
Begin with you.
Let me show you how.

Exercise: Begin Within

For this exercise I want you to take a pen and paper to the place where you feel most comfortable. This might be your bedroom or any other room in your home, it might be sitting under a shade tree, the beach or any number of places where you are undisturbed and can connect to your spiritual self. Once you get to this place I want you to answer the following questions honestly and openly. If you're afraid that someone might see what you write down then shred, burn or flush the paper after the exercise is completed. While you're answering these questions don't just write yes or no, but elaborate on each one. You might be surprised at what you discover about yourself when you read it back.

- Do I love myself? Why or Why not. (List reasons for your answer.)
- Has my self-esteem been negatively affected by another person?
- Can I release my feelings about past events with this other person and raise my self esteem?
- Can I forgive the person and move forward in my life? Why or

why not?
- Have I wronged someone else in the same manner?
- Do I feel guilty for anything in my life? Explain.
- Can I forgive myself and move forward? Why or why not?
- Am I accepting responsibility for my own actions?
- Am I connected to my spiritual self?
- Do I feel spiritual gratitude deep within, at a spiritual level, or do I give it just a passing thought?
- What are the gifts that I'm given when I am spiritually grateful?
- Am I restricting myself from receiving these gifts?
- Am I committed to living in spiritual gratitude and embracing the happiness and joy that it will bring into my life?
- If not, what's holding me back from loving myself and living in spiritual gratitude?

Once you have answered all of these questions honestly and thoughtfully, you will be able to have a better grasp on where you stand right now and hone in on any areas where you can improve. Addressing issues at the beginning of living in thankfulness can help you embrace spiritual gratitude and loving yourself.

Defining Spiritual Gratitude

I gave you a definition for spiritual gratitude earlier so now let's look at the difference in spiritual gratitude and just being thankful for things? Gratitude is when you have feelings of thankfulness and appreciation for the good things in your life. These are physical things that you have like a job, a car, or a home. It also includes people connections like your family, significant other, friends or acquaintances. Then there are the good experiences that you have, for instance, when someone treats you fairly, or is kind to you, or helps you in some way. Having enough money to support your lifestyle, feeling grateful when things work out the way you planned or being thankful when everything is going well in your life are also examples of thankfulness. Spiritual gratitude is when you feel these same emotions of thankfulness at a much deeper level, at your soul essence, when you live in thankfulness daily because it is part of who you are within your soul. It is sharing feelings of thankfulness with others.

For example, when you express gratitude do you give thanks with conditions attached? Do you say *thank you but…*? Or maybe you are using words of gratitude to pat yourself on the back, using your materialistic accomplishments in order to praise yourself? That's acting in a self-serving way, which spiritual gratitude is not. If you're always wanting more than you have and feel negatively when you don't get it, then you aren't showing appreciation for what you do have. Do you tend to take things for granted? If you do, then you may forget to be thankful for them. Expressing spiritual gratitude can be challenging, but if you develop it into a habit, it soon becomes second nature.

Sometimes feelings of inadequacy can affect your ability to feel spiritual gratitude. You may think that the only reason someone helped you was because they thought you couldn't do it for yourself. In this instance, try thinking about the person's actions from their point of view. Maybe it had nothing to do with whether you could or could not do it for yourself and had everything to do with their own feelings of thankfulness for you just being in their life. Maybe helping you made *them* feel more worthwhile and good about themselves. For this, you should be grateful instead of looking for an ulterior motive behind the person's actions. Try not to let any negative feelings or suspicions you may have impact your appreciation for acts of kindness from a fellow human being.

Spiritual gratitude begins deep within your soul essence and encompasses thankfulness on a Universal level. It is unconditional appreciation with no strings attached. It is when you are thankful for everything in your life, from the smallest to the largest and everything in-between. Spiritual gratitude is all encompassing, it is thankfulness for everything that affects or doesn't affect you both directly and indirectly. Spiritual gratitude is an interconnectedness of all energy within the Universe. Whether its world events or just the fact that you woke up this morning.

Spiritual gratitude is feeling appreciation for all that is, all that was, and all that will ever be. It's thankfulness of being, of consciousness, and of the divine.

When you are spiritually grateful, you may notice that you're more connected to the divine, to your own spiritual being, to the energy of other people and all things within the world around you. You feel more in tune with the Universe, which can propel you along your spiritual path and bring more divine light into your life. This leads to more joy and happiness, a clearer understanding of your life purpose. You may change your point of view as you gain more clarity of spirit and become more open to new ideas that you previously wouldn't have even considered.

When you start consciously practicing spiritual gratitude you might still forget at times but that's okay. As long as you're making continued strides forward then you'll experience an increase in positivity in all areas of your life.

Positive and negative energies are in every living thing and inanimate object within the Universe. Being spiritually grateful doesn't mean that you fully accept the positive and deny the negative. We want to feel positivity to live happy, fulfilled lives by staying clear of negativity. That's an excellent goal to strive towards, however; you will always encounter negativity in some form from others or within yourself. It's how you react to and counter this negativity with your own positive energy when you come across it that matters.

In moving toward the goal of living a more positive, grateful life you also have to recognize and acknowledge your own negative feelings. Are you sad, lonely, frustrated or mad at the world? When you face these emotions, look for their source and understand why you feel this way. Once you have a handle on why you're feeling these emotions then you can embrace them with spiritual gratitude and learn something from them. When you are spiritually grateful, these negative emotions can change to positive ones through understanding and thankfulness.

Spiritual gratitude is living in the moment, in the now of your life, without regrets for anything in your past whether it involves your own actions or the actions of another. Living in spiritual gratitude helps you to release old ties, patterns of negativity and to take pleasure in each moment that you live, without worry about what will happen tomorrow. It is being consciously aware of each minute and second of your life. When you focus spiritually on giving thanks for whatever it is you're thankful for, you immerse yourself so totally into that feeling of gratefulness that negativity slips away. There are no worries about tomorrow and no regrets about yesterday. There is only your complete feeling of appreciation that connects you to Universal Energy and gives you a sense of oneness with all that is. Allow yourself to become immersed in your experiences, fully appreciate them and feel the happiness they bring to your life.

Create a New You by Awakening to Spiritual Gratitude

Now I know you just finished a big exercise but before we get into the depths of this book, I want you to do one more. And don't worry—after this they'll only be one or two per chapter—I'm not going to exercise you to death. So go grab a pen and a piece of paper and make a list of everything that you're grateful for in your life. Run along now. I'll wait right here and sip my coffee until you're finished.

All done? Great!

If you didn't make your list, stop reading and make it right now, before we go any further. The only way you can understand and develop your sense of spiritual gratitude is to know what you're grateful for in your life. It does take a little work on your part to awaken to spiritual gratitude.

When you've finished the list, take a close look at what you've written down. Do you notice that you're more thankful for the physical things in your life, the people in your life, your career, or the spiritual? Let's take this one step further. On a separate piece of paper, make columns for each main category (physical, people, career, spiritual or other main topic you come up with) and then copy the individual entries onto this new sheet of paper and place each item in the appropriate column, one per line. Now look at the columns. Is there balance or are all the things you're thankful for in one column? By doing this type of analysis, you can start to become more aware of the areas where you are very grateful and other areas where you should be more thankful. When you see it on paper like this, it's easier to bring yourself into balance because you can see exactly the areas where you don't express as much gratitude. Since you've got the hang of this, now that you've made and analyzed your first spiritual gratitude list, try to make it a habit to write down the things you're spiritually grateful for each day.

Spiritual gratitude is like a living thing. It grows and manifests your desires because as you give thanks, you are putting out positive energy into the Universe and that energy will come back to you. To begin living in spiritual gratitude make it a practice to write down at least three things that you're grateful for each morning and then add to your list throughout the day. At the end of the day, review your list. Does anything on it surprise you? Can you relate anything that happened during the day to the things on your list? For instance, if you wrote down that you were grateful for the mail being delivered in a timely manner, and then you unexpectedly received a letter from someone you haven't heard from in a while, then that's a connection to your thankfulness and receiving positivity in return. It may not happen this quickly, but you get the idea.

At its core spiritual gratitude is self-improvement through the connection to your soul and feelings of thankfulness. I believe that the word *spiritual* doesn't refer to any specific religion but is instead the essence of your spirit and the way you feel about things on a soul level. You can be a member of any religious belief system; you can have even made up your own religious beliefs because it is your own spirituality that is important here. It's your soul energy, how you connect to your core being and higher self. To me the word spiritual goes beyond any specific religion to encompass all that is and all that will ever be in this world and in the spiritual realm. It is your truth, essence and light. Spiritual gratitude is thankfulness in everything. When you combine these two, then spiritual gratitude is giving thanks in everything from the core essence of your true spiritual self.

When you practice spiritual gratitude in your life then you are awakening your soul and you can create a *new you* simply through awareness and positive change. You are moving from a state of negativity to positivity or from a positive place to an even higher plane of positivity. You are learning about who you are at your spiritual essence and connecting to your spiritual self. This doesn't mean that you'll suddenly become a person who never experiences negativity. Life can be trying at times and we all have days where we just feel down and out. But if you're making an effort to be spiritually grateful in your life, then those days happen less often. When bad things happen, you're better able to handle them because you're thinking and reacting in spiritual gratitude, which is a higher plane.

Everyone needs to vent sometimes, or to blow off steam or cry on someone's shoulder. That's human nature and it's healthier to let it all out then to keep it all bottled up inside of you because eventually you'll explode if you don't. As long as you are like a teapot and blow off steam, then simmer back down, while not hurting anyone in the process, then you should have moments like this. Scream into your pillow, punch it or cry into it and as soon as your emotional outburst is over, express your thanks for the experience and move on. No one is perfect and no one should expect you to be perfect, including yourself. It is in our imperfection that we can learn to be humble and filled with love and joy.

Spiritual gratitude links you to the Divine. Once developed and embraced it becomes a way of life because you've integrated it into your core essence and made it a habit, part of your daily routine. With it comes a new state of mind, where you no longer dwell on the negative but will instead look for the good things in life and be grateful for whatever comes your way. It helps you make sense of every aspect of your life because you now look at the good more than the problems. You'll no longer take things for granted but will appreciate all that life has to offer. You can leave negative traits like greediness and jealousy behind and embrace giving, contentment and appreciation. When you awaken to spiritual gratitude and apply it to your life, you become more understanding. So step out of your comfort zone and analyze yourself as honestly as you can then take the necessary steps to become a more joyful person through the simple act of being spiritually grateful.

Shifting from Ingratitude to Spiritual Gratitude

Ingratitude is when you are ungrateful, when you don't show appreciation for the people and things in your life. It is when you feel that people owe you something, when you never feel that you have enough, when you complain and whine constantly, instead of looking positively at your life.

You've probably met people like this at some point. They're always whining, never thankful, and always want you to do more and more for them, and it's never enough, no matter how hard you try to make them happy.

Don't confuse an ungrateful whiner with someone just telling you about their experiences. While you may think their experience sounds like a problem or difficulty, they see it as a normal part of their day.

Let me give you an example that I've had happen to me. I have quite a few animals that will hurt themselves one way or the other, no matter how much I try to protect them. Why? Because they're animals, it's what they do. They don't think of the consequences of running into the fence head first or know that rubbing against the tree to scratch an itch will take out chunks of mane or when you escape your dog kennel it can result in cuts and stitches. When I tell people about my latest animal antics, sometimes they think it's horrible what I've gone through and feel sorry for me, to which I quickly reply that I'm not complaining, just telling them about it and that these types of things are part of my normal day. Sometimes the things they do can be really funny (think grown stallion trying to nurse a mare who just had a foal – she looked at him like he was crazy!). If you don't have animals, you may not realize that this is just a normal situation.

So if someone is telling you something that you think is negative, consider if it's normal for them and they're just telling you something they experienced that day, or if they're indeed whining about "poor-pitiful-me" and being ungrateful. Once you've made that decision, you decide how to react.

If you do find yourself dealing with an ungrateful whiner, the best thing to do is to be thankful for the person and then step back, letting them stand on their own two feet, to learn to act on their own. It's tough love to help someone begin to look at the positives in life and to see themselves as they truly are. Sometimes, when you do things for someone for too long of a time, when you hold their hand instead of letting them walk on their own, even if they stumble and fall, then you're enabling their ungratefulness. They start to believe that they deserve what you're doing for them, that they don't have to be grateful for you or what you do because they are entitled to it. Take a lesson from this type of behavior. How do you feel when you're unappreciated, when others don't thank you after you've taken extra time to help them with something or when you've given them a gift? It doesn't feel very good does it?

To determine if you're ungrateful you have to look inside of yourself. Unfortunately, in this day and age, many people feel such a sense of entitlement, as if someone owes them something just because they exist, that ungratefulness is running amuck in our society. There are ways to tell if you're being ungrateful. You have to look at your actions, reactions and feelings. You have to examine yourself at your spiritual core because only you know how you feel about things. In order to experience more spiritual gratitude, you have to start by acknowledging areas where you feel ingratitude, where you are not expressing your spiritual gratitude, and where you feel entitled or that you deserve something when in actuality that's not true.

Being ungrateful is a character flaw that you often don't see in yourself (unless you look for it) but everyone around you is aware of. Most people don't like to be around someone who is ungrateful because it is considered a negative behavior that can become very annoying. You can bring other people down, make them upset or irritated, simply by your ungrateful actions. Is that really the type of person you want to be?

It is human nature for us to feel ungrateful sometimes, despite our best efforts otherwise, but when you wallow in it, then it can have a negative effect on your own energy over time. If you change your thoughts, you'll change actions, and that can change your life. You will switch from feelings of ungratefulness to feelings of spiritual gratitude and you'll draw more positive energy to you which will allow you to see life in an optimistic way. It's like looking at the glass as half-full or half-empty. If you're ungrateful you'll see it as half-empty but if you're grateful you'll see it as half-full.

In order to be spiritually grateful you have to purposefully move away from ingratitude toward spiritual gratitude. If you're not accustomed to being grateful, you have to start a little at a time. If you simply decide one day that you'll be spiritually grateful for everything, then it'll be too overwhelming and it'll be easier to give up before you even get started. Take baby steps and begin within.

Are you grateful for yourself? Do you appreciate your own spiritual being? If you don't, then you have to change how you think about yourself. What is your life purpose? Are you a teacher or a caregiver? Take a few minutes to really think about this. Look at your deepest beliefs, your values, and code of ethics. Consider what is most important to you. Look at how these interconnect with your essence. What do you see? This is the real you, the person that you came to the earthly plane to be. Have you strayed from your true self, your purpose and essence through spiritual gratitude? If so, take back control.

Start by looking at that list I asked you to make at the beginning of this book. Look at the columns that don't have many things listed in it. Now think about yourself while I give you an example. Are you ungrateful at work because you're frustrated with your co-workers? Then that's a place to start. Instead of letting them frustrate you, try taking a step back and look at them as if you don't know them. What do you see? Are they sad, angry, or overly helpful? Do they need to be in control? Find at least one aspect about each co-worker's personality that you can appreciate. Once you do that, look at them a little deeper and try to see the divine within them. Can you find one grain of positivity within them that you can be grateful for? If you're having trouble finding something, then start with this—they are just like you—a soul who has come to the early plane in order to experience events that will teach them lessons so that they can return to God (regardless of the name they use for God, even if it's different than the one you use). Like you, they face challenges, and they have fears, worries and hardships.

For instance, if someone is controlling at work, could it be because they have a loss of control at home? As you look for the divine spiritual person that your co-workers are within, imagine feeling their light shining upon you. How does it make you feel? Can you be more grateful for them now that you've looked for their soul essence? Think about how they influence you when you're not feeling frustrated by their actions. If you could simply recognize the divine light within them, then any frustrations you feel can be eased or completely released.

As you learn to release your frustrations with your co-workers and become more spiritually grateful for them, you'll find that situations at work tend to go more smoothly because you appreciate those you work with more. It may be an amazing change for you. Why? It is because you're looking at the situation, your job, through eyes of spiritual gratitude instead of ingratitude, you're seeing work and the people you work with in a whole different light. You're no longer focusing on the negative in the workplace or what you're ungrateful for, but in changing your attitude by becoming more grateful, you've in effect changed the energy surrounding your job. You've transformed what was frustrating you into a positive experience simply by changing the way you look at it. This type of transformation can take place in any aspect of your life when you shift away from ingratitude to spiritual gratitude and simply give thanks. All you have to do is want this positive change and do the work to achieve it.

Spiritual Gratitude and Unhappiness Can't Co-exist

Spiritual gratitude can't co-exist with misery nor can it co-exist if you're harboring resentment, feeling victimized or living in fear. Sure, you can laugh and cry at the same time but usually when this happens, they are tears of joy. Spiritual gratitude can't co-exist with negativity because as you become thankful for the negatives in your life, you take away any power the negative things have over you and release them. That in itself is pretty powerful.

Spiritual gratitude is a level of happiness because you're showing your appreciation for the things that you feel, experience, and come into contact with through your connection to Spirit, your soul and Universal energy. It's difficult to be happy and unhappy at the same time in the same place within the same being. Spiritual gratitude, when practiced daily can transform your feelings of unhappiness to unlimited feelings of joy.

You have to experience spiritual gratitude for yourself in order to make this happen. You can be grateful for things that happened in the past but you can't be grateful for things that haven't happened yet, so feeling spiritual gratitude, happiness and joy is something that happens in the moment, in the now of your life. Choose to see the glass as half-full, find that silver lining in the clouds and be appreciative of the fact that you are living life. When you're happy, unhappiness drifts away. When you're grateful, you're happier.

Harboring resentment against others can turn into bitterness in a hurry. When you're resentful and bitter, you aren't allowing yourself to experience the good things you encounter. You're placing blame on someone else instead of taking responsibility for your own life. When you can't let go of past hurts and blame someone else's actions on your current behavior, then you're wallowing in negativity and self-pity, you do not grow spiritually and your divine light doesn't shine as brightly. No one wants to be around people like this because they get tired of always hearing the negative talk. People who harbor resentment often never have anything positive to say because they're too focused on complaining about the reasons they're bitter and resentful. They often blame a person or situation for their resentment. For example, let's say they lost their job as a stage hand for a famous band that they adored but the person they were dating got to stay on with the group. The couple broke up and since that time the person left behind has grown to hate music in general and is resentful against the person they'd been dating because they continued with the band. They feel as if they were cheated and have hung on to those resentful feelings for years. If instead, the person expressed gratefulness toward the situation, and looked at the positives in their life that they may not have had if they'd stayed with the band, then they could see the good and leave this in the past where it belongs. When you're spiritually grateful, you will not harbor resentment against others or your life experiences but will see them as a stepping stone to where you are at in your life now. It will be easier to understand that staying with the band wasn't part of your path in life. In the light of spiritual gratitude, resentment cannot thrive.

Are you feeling victimized? Do you often think *poor, pitiful me?* When hardships abound it is easy to think that you're a victim of your surroundings or of your life. That it's your *destiny* to be a victim at the mercy of others. If you're feeling like a victim, then look for why you're feeling that way. Is there a problem at work, are you having money problems or arguments with your significant other that are making you feel this way? Notice when you are feeling victimized and then replace the feeling of being a victim with spiritual gratitude and give thanks that you have a job to go to every day, that you are making enough money to live and that you have a significant other to argue with. When you look at these things from an attitude of spiritual gratitude, then you aren't going to feel like a victim any longer. You will begin to notice that if you start to feel like a victim, you're actually withdrawing within yourself because you're not thinking clearly about the situation. When you look at it instead with spiritual gratitude, then you're seeing the situation as it is, without letting your feelings interfere. You can then be thankful for the situation and know that positive energy will keep you from feeling victimized by it.

Living in fear can be utterly self-destructive on a soul level. When you are spiritually grateful, you can release the fear that is holding you back from being your true spiritual self. It may not be easy to do since facing fear is a challenging situation simply because you are afraid. In order to allow spiritual gratitude to erase the fear in your life, you first have to recognize what is causing it. Then, acknowledge the value in that reason, (whether you like it or not), and release it by expressing your thanks for it. Let's say you have an ungrounded fear of the dark. Maybe this fear started when you were a child when you imagined there were monsters under your bed. As you grew up, you just couldn't find a way to let go of that fear. Now, instead of being afraid, you have to face that fear because you'll always have to deal with the night. Understand that night is as much a part of life as the daylight is and be thankful for it. Appreciate that you're able to sleep better in the darkness and know that things are the same in your room at night as they are in the daytime. Let this thankfulness eliminate the fear you've previously experienced. If you're having trouble moving past the fear of monsters under your bed, then put the mattress on the floor until spiritual gratitude can help you release the fear. If there isn't a space between the bed and the floor there's nowhere for the monster to live is there? Expressing spiritual gratitude toward things that challenge us enables us to transform it from a negative to a positive. In this case, you can't be afraid of the dark if you're thankful for it and understand that it is a normal part of our natural world.

Daily Practice Is Important

How do you know where to start when it comes to practicing spiritual gratitude? How do you even begin to turn things around? You do this by starting where you are today, right at this very minute. Pull out your list again and take a close look at it. Where can you be more grateful? Do you need to be more grateful at work? Or do you need to show more appreciation for your family? Maybe you're developing your spiritual gifts but your progress is slow because you're not being thankful for them along the way. The important thing is to remember to practice gratitude every day, even if it's in a small way, so that it becomes a habit. And is one of the best, most constructive habits you could ever develop for yourself.

If you can only see the negatives in your life because everything has been going wrong for so long that you're surrounded by negativity in mind, body and soul, then just take it one day at a time, one hour at a time, and one minute at a time. Think of things that *didn't* happen to you today. Maybe work was horrible but you drove there and back home safely without getting into a car accident. That's something to be thankful for. Maybe you dropped a glass and it broke into a million pieces that you had to clean up—which was annoying because you broke one of your best glasses—but you didn't cut your hand. You can be grateful for that, right? Or maybe your sister called you out of the blue just to see how you were doing. Don't you feel happy and grateful that she was thinking of you and now you get to talk to her? Start with little things like this and practice feeling spiritual gratitude towards them as they happen to you.

During the day try to think of what you're grateful for every time you remember that you're practicing spiritual gratitude. Because you're busy, you'll remember that you're being more spiritually grateful at random times throughout the day, possibly when you have a negative thought or experience, so when you remember, just take a minute to appreciate one or two things that you can be grateful for at that exact moment in time. Be appreciative in the *now* of your day. You can access spiritual gratitude at any point in the day or night, whenever you think about it, whenever you feel the need to grow as a person or let go of negative feelings and replace them with joyful appreciation.

The more you practice spiritual gratitude, the stronger its influence; the happier you'll become and the more joy you'll feel in life. Don't give up if the process seems difficult but keep moving forward. If you forget to be consciously grateful one day, that's okay, just start again the next day or whenever you remember. Don't beat yourself up when you forget. It is part of the normal process of creating a habit and you will forget sometimes. Be thankful that you remembered and at that moment, mentally make a list of the things you've experienced up until that point in the day. It's the act of expressing your emotions of spiritual gratitude that is important even if you can't write them down or forget to do it for a while.

It may be easier for you when starting out if you keep a spiritual gratitude journal. This way you can carry it with you and jot down notes to yourself when you're feeling grateful. You can make your daily list on one page and follow up on the next page by expressing your feelings about how being spiritually grateful did or didn't work for you that day. If you're not the journaling type, then think about what you're grateful for at a specific time of day. Maybe you can do this as you're getting ready for the day, while you're showering or on your commute to or from work. If you prefer to talk then speak your list into a hand held recorder, or if you prefer electronics create a note on your computer or smart phone.

As with any habit that you're trying to create—the more you do it, the easier it becomes. Let's say you're trying to do one hundred sit-ups a day. You may start with only two or three if you're really out of shape, but the more that you practice, the more you're able to do until pretty soon you're hitting the goal of one hundred sit-ups every day. With spiritual gratitude, the more you practice it, the more benefits you'll receive. Over time you'll notice that not only do you feel more joy and happiness but you feel more alive and in sync with the world. There will be less times of distress and more moments of pleasure.

Don't wait until something good happens in your life to be grateful. Spiritual gratitude will change the way you look at things so if you practice it daily, even when something good hasn't happened yet, then you're attracting good things to you. You are creating an abundance of positivity, manifesting it and drawing it to your energy simply by giving thanks on a spiritual level for everything that is. Do not put limits on your spiritual gratitude but let it be all encompassing.

Just as you have a particular routine that you follow during your day, make a routine that you can follow when practicing spiritual gratitude. If you typically wake up early, check your email, shower, dress, have breakfast, brush your teeth and then leave for work, why not add making a spiritual gratitude list after you check your email? If you're not a routine kind of person, then randomly practice spiritual gratitude throughout the day to reap its bountiful rewards on your path of spiritual growth and development. Your reward will be a happy life filled with joy and contentment on every level.

—2—
Spiritual Gratitude and Soul Purpose

Living in spiritual gratitude keeps you on your divine pathway and can help you move forward in positivity, with purpose and joy. When practiced consciously and consistently, spiritual gratitude is powerful. You will notice that positivity is drawn to you in abundance and when positive things come to you in life then happiness follows.

The connection between spiritual gratitude and the soul's purpose is complete oneness between your true essence and spirituality. When you are truly grateful, and I don't mean just a quick half-hearted thank you in passing for something you received, but a true deeply felt emotion of sincere spiritual gratitude that comes from the depths of your soul and from your heart, then these emotions serve as the catalyst that can transform your life to greater heights of oneness. You will experience a greater sense of purpose in your life and joy in that purpose. When you choose to initiate spiritual gratitude in your life, you are choosing to allow positivity to become part of your spiritual essence. Spiritual gratitude is all about your perception of life. The choice is yours. When you are grateful for all that you have in your life, then you attract more positive, wonderful people, situations and blessings to come to you.

Be Authentic and True to Your Soul's Purpose

The *purpose* of your soul is the quest that you are on in this lifetime. It is the reason you were born on the earthly plane of existence and it contains the biggest lesson that you will learn during your time here. You will have many lessons in your lifetime because every experience brings the opportunity to learn from life. If you don't know what your soul's purpose is, take a moment to think about it. Are you here to be a teacher to others? Are you a caregiver? Maybe your soul's purpose is to protect. There are many, many purposes and there is one unique to your soul, to your path and to your spirituality. As you consider your soul's purpose, also consider your past. Can you find a pattern of behavior that sheds some illumination on your soul's purpose?

The biggest step you can take in being true to your soul's purpose in this lifetime is to be authentically yourself at all times. Don't be fickle. You know what you like, what you don't like, what you believe and what you don't believe. It doesn't matter if others don't share your likes, dislikes or beliefs because they are on their own path, not yours. Even though your path may feel difficult at times, being true to your purpose is how you will ensure that you learn your lessons and grow spiritually.

Let me give you an example. For years, I denied my intuitive abilities simply because I didn't know what to do with them and frankly, sometimes they scared me. I was afraid of what other people thought. I didn't like being called names or being made fun of because I knew things that were going to happen. So, I pushed the abilities to the background and ignored them, chalking up most things to coincidence. After years of denial, and the abilities and experiences not going away, I finally gave up. It was too hard to keep denying what was part of my soul's purpose. Once I embraced my abilities, started publically doing readings for others and sharing what I had experienced, it felt as if I was finally *home* spiritually. I felt an inner peace that wasn't present when I was constantly pushing my abilities and paranormal experiences away. For years I said, "I never asked to have these things happen to me" but now I know that I did ask for the experiences but I had to learn the hard way in order to teach others.

When you are authentic to your soul's purpose, regardless of what that purpose is, you will find that life is easier, you feel content and happy within yourself, even during hard times. Being true to yourself isn't always easy but it is always rewarding.

There are other steps you can take to unveil your soul's purpose if it is unclear to you. As you take these steps don't make this more complicated than it needs to be. When you try too hard, then you can block your path. Remember too that your life lesson doesn't always have to be something that is difficult. It can be very easy for you once you recognize it. Your soul's purpose in this lifetime doesn't always have to be that of struggle and difficulties but can in fact be something pleasant, fun, and easy to accomplish. As you set forth to discover your soul's purpose, keep this in mind.

Exercise: Find Your Soul Purpose

I love lists. I have lists for everything because they help keep me organized. Even if I don't have a list written down, I have one running through my head of the things I need to do. Right now I want you to make another list, which will help you discover your soul's purpose. When you write down what I ask of you, make the list from the heart. Don't write what you think others expect of you or what you've been told you should do by your parents or significant other, instead, write down what you feel in your heart of hearts. Write down that which resonates within you as *your* truth. In doing this, you'll find your soul's purpose. Now I'd like for you to answer the following questions:

1. What do you like to do the most on a daily basis?
2. Take question 1 a step further – if you were so rich that money wasn't an obstacle – what would you choose to do on a daily basis? Would you travel, work out, visit hospitals and spend time with patients, train animals, work in a rescue etc? Really think about this question because it may be very different than number one now that you have unlimited funds.
3. What are some of the things you feel that you're really good at?
4. Take 3 a step further – what are some of the things that other people think you excel at? These might be completely different than your list.
5. What are your talents?
6. Take five a step further - What do others tell you are your talents?
7. Think about your past and the things you excelled at, or that you really enjoyed doing during your lifetime that you may or may not currently do.

Now that you've made your list it's time to examine it. I asked you to write down what others say about you not because you will base your final decision as to your soul purpose on what they say, but because sometimes we can't see our own talents as clearly as other people see them. Go through your list and notice any recurring themes or talents. You may even notice that your soul's purpose is threefold – no one said we can only have one purpose in life.

There is no wrong answer here. Your soul's purpose is exactly that—*your* soul's purpose. What is right for you is uniquely your path to follow, and you may also notices changes in your path during your lifetime. If you're experiencing joy, fulfillment, happiness and a calm inner peace within you as you live your life in spiritual gratitude, then you are living authentically true to your soul's purpose.

It's Not About the Money or Material Things

While you should be thankful for the money you earn and the things you're able to buy with that money, those are just material items. Sometimes, when you focus too much on the material you can lose focus on the spiritual part of your essence. When you think of simply giving thanks, include the material things that you're thankful for but don't let them consume you. With thankfulness, you should be able to find a balance between the material, the spiritual, the people in your life and everything for which you're grateful. When you focus your thankfulness in only one area then you're out of balance spiritually. It is easy to stay in balance when you view thankfulness in this way and don't view spiritual gratitude as something that applies only to material possessions.

Spiritual gratitude and your soul's purpose are connected because each one enhances the other. We are each born with our own individual paths to follow and our own reason for being. If you're still unsure after doing the previous exercise, there are some other things you can do to discover why you are here. Think about the things you are passionate about, the things you really enjoy doing in your life that makes you truly happy. What are the things that really excite you, that make you feel *alive*?

What drives you in life? I'm not talking about your job. Your job is what you do to make a living and it can be an expression of your soul's purpose in some way but it might not be either.

Let's look at an example. Maybe you earn a living as a factory worker but outside of work, you're really enthusiastic about sports, building things or photography. Taking the time to join a team, to build something or to take pictures may require more energy than your job, may be more challenging on an emotional level, but it gives you a sense of peace and accomplishment. You feel happy and energized to do this work, even if you don't think of it as work, because you look forward to it and enjoy it. Doing these things is part of your soul's purpose—it's who you are deep inside. It's something that, if you weren't doing them, then you would feel unfulfilled in life. By sharing of your true soul essence you are giving of yourself by helping another being by being part of a team, building something for someone else or through sharing your talents as a photographer with others.

If you find that you're feeling unfulfilled then take a good look at what you're thankful for, what drives you and the direction your life is taking. Are you utilizing your talents at a soul level? If not, then make a list of the things that you really like to do, what you have to offer humankind through your talents or skills. Think about this: if you were to share those talents and skills, would you feel more fulfilled? If the answer is yes, then it's time to make some changes in your life.

That which makes you happiest will probably have nothing to do with earning money or the material things that you have in your life. Sure, money makes life easier and having nice things is great, but it's not the only thing in life. In our society it's very easy to get caught up in keeping up with Joneses or thinking that you must have this or that to be truly happy. When you're in a mad race to earn enough money to get this or that then you might also very well forget to be thankful along the way. You might miss the little things in life that you're thankful for because you're taking them for granted.

What would happen if you decided to take a completely opposite approach and simplify your life? Would you be appreciative of having more time to do the things that really resonate with you and make you happy? Someone once asked me, "What would you do with your life if money wasn't an issue?" It was such a great question that I asked you to include it in your own list in the last exercise. Take a minute to really think about it again now. I actually thought about it for about a week. If you had an unlimited bank account, how would you spend your time? You could go anywhere and do anything that your heart desires. The answers that you come up with might actually surprise and amaze you. They can give you insight into what you're thankful for and will also bring you closer to your soul's purpose. When you think of what you'd do if you didn't have to go to work and earn a living, then you're considering what brings you happiness, things you'd enjoy doing and accomplishments that you'd want for yourself. This question really does change your outlook.

As you're becoming more aware of your soul's purpose and the things in life that you're thankful for, take money and material possessions off the list. Instead look at your relationships with your family and friends. Are you spending time with them? Are you grateful for them? If you're too wrapped up with earning a living, can you do something to change that and make time for others in your life? Are you being the person that you really want to be or are you going through the motions because you're so busy being the person that you have to be? Are you neglecting your own health? Imagine yourself years in the future, thinking back on your life as it is now. Thinking as an older version of yourself, is there something you see that you would do differently? I always say that you can get a good perspective on situations you're going through if you look at them as an outsider watching what is happening in your life. This is the same principle, but you're looking back as an older version of yourself. If you see something you would change, then make that change now. Then, when you are that older you, you'll have fewer regrets, if any.

Remember too that you can't take money or material things with you when you pass. But you will take love and for that you can be thankful.

Don't Let Ingratitude Destroy Your Soul Purpose

Ingratitude is the lack of thankfulness in your life and it can destroy your soul's purpose because it is in direct opposition to your true soul essence. We are spiritually grateful beings but when life gives us challenges and lessons to learn that seem negative, its human nature to say, "Why is this happening to me?" Challenges can turn you sour and ungrateful, if you look at the situations you find yourself in negatively instead of positively. It can become a vicious cycle. The more you notice the negatives, the more you become ungrateful and the more you become ungrateful, the more you notice the negatives in life. Instead of allowing yourself to fall into this pattern, make a conscious effort to practice thankfulness and spiritual gratitude on a daily basis.

How do you know if you're being ungrateful? Do you feel slighted if you aren't appreciated for your hard work? Is there something you can do to change this? Of course there is! It may not be easy to do but when you're feeling unappreciated, sometimes you just have to let the situation go. Know in your heart that what you did was worthwhile even if it wasn't noticed or appreciated by someone else. Their reaction or non-reaction doesn't mean that you can't appreciate yourself for doing a good job. You can and you should! If you stepped up to bat when someone else wouldn't or helped someone out when they had a problem that they couldn't solve but you could solve for them—even if you didn't have time, and they patronized you and were ungrateful for your help in the end—then just let it go. Know that you did a good deed and the negative is on them, not you. There are a lot of people in the world who thrive off of their own ego because they think they know everything and are always right, even when they're wrong, but you don't have let them affect your own sense of self-worth through their negativity or their own ingratitude. This might even mean cutting ties with the person, which is something only you can decide, but sometimes, the headaches aren't worth the connections.

Ingratitude can really pull your frequency (your soul's vibrational rate) down. Experiencing ingratitude at the hands of someone else can make you feel angry, sad, slighted, or depressed if you let it. But you don't have to let it. You can give thanks for them anyway. Be thankful that you were able to experience their ingratitude because it will make you more aware of your own feelings of spiritual gratitude. When you are thankful for them and for the experience that you had with them, then you are reversing the energy associated with the situation. Being grateful fills you with a sense of peace and brings balance to your frequency and can even elevate it. If you're feeling challenged by ingratitude, then make a point to counter it with thankfulness, appreciation, and love to turn your feelings about the situation around.

But what if you're the one feeling ungrateful? How can you release the feelings of ingratitude and embrace thankfulness? You can do this by reconnecting with your soul's purpose. Take a minute to consider the wonderful people in your life, the blessings that you've been given and the happiness you feel when you think of the good around you instead of what has made you feel ingratitude. Do you have a best friend that will listen while you vent it all out and empathize with you? That person is someone you can be truly grateful for. Ingratitude usually stems from a negative experience and it's often felt because of the actions of another. As spiritual beings with a soul purpose, we're naturally grateful, until outside forces affect us negatively.

We've all experienced ingratitude from others at some point in our lives and we've all felt ungrateful at some time. It's what you do with the feeling that's important. You can choose to remain ungrateful or you can choose to release it and return to thankfulness by reconnecting to your true essence and reversing your feelings of ingratitude. It really is all about choice.

Ingratitude can destroy your soul's purpose in several ways. First, it is a very negative way to think and feel. It is normal, from a soul perspective, to feel spiritual gratitude in all that is. This includes both the positive and the negative that we encounter. By going against the grain of what is naturally a part of our soul essence, we are creating negativity within, which can eat away at your soul's purpose and make you forget why you're here. Secondly, when you are ungrateful, it is difficult to see your inner self and your purpose. You can become so blinded by the negative feelings associated with ingratitude that you only focus on why everything is always going wrong or why people don't treat you the way you feel you should be treated; the list can go on and on. When you change your attitude and practice thankfulness in every aspect of your life, then you are moving past being immersed in ingratitude to being filled with thankfulness. And lastly, ingratitude can destroy your soul's purpose because it can lower your frequency, your personal vibrational rate, to extremely low levels. When your frequency is low, you can have a plethora of problems and you will have to work hard to get it back to a higher level through thankfulness.

As you reconnect to your soul's purpose, your true divine calling in life, you will experience not only inner peace but an overwhelming sense of gratitude for all that you have experienced. Life is full of lessons and one of those lessons (that I think applies to just about everyone) is how to overcome the ingratitude of others and reawaken to our own sense of thankfulness during challenging times. You can do this by looking within yourself, by analyzing the situation and any other people involved. Then, you can choose to follow your own individual path in accordance with your soul's lessons on this spiritual journey we call life.

Do and Be What You Believe

Living your life in its truest form means doing and being what you believe deep within your soul. When you are one with your soul purpose, then you'll find that life is flowing in an easy rhythm. If you're not at this place yet, you'll notice that all sorts of things can pop up out of the blue just to throw you off course. I believe this is actually your soul frequency, your guides and the Universe trying to steer you back on course to reconnect with your soul purpose. If you find that this often happens to you, then it's time to take a deeper look within to discover why your life feels out of sync.

From birth until death, your life is a mission. It may take you a while to uncover exactly what that mission is, but when you do, you may also realize that what you've learned up to the point of discovery—your skills, the development of your abilities, and your remembrance of your soul's path—were all part of the plan. For some of us it takes years to get to the point of discovery, while for others it happens relatively quickly. Have you ever known a kid who knew exactly what they were going to be when they grew up and then , as an adult, worked in that job? The career was part of that person's soul purpose and they realized it at a young age.

When you align with your soul's purpose it is easier to do the things you believe in because you know deep inside that you're supposed to be doing them. You can be your soul self. You can live life according to your beliefs because they are an integral part of you. Spiritual gratitude can give you a clear outlook of your life and can clear the way to see your soul's purpose. We are emotional beings and if you're not doing and being what you believe, then you can put emotional roadblocks in your own path. By experiencing spiritual gratitude for all that you are and all that you can be, you can move those roadblocks out of your way.

I like giving examples because I feel they can help to see situations in a different light. For this example, I'll use myself. When my abilities first appeared in my life I was unsure of what to make of them. At first I thought they were really cool but then the more I used them, the stronger they got and I became afraid of them. I didn't want to see people who had already died. I didn't want to know things before they happened so the best thing to do (to my young mind) was to totally shut the door on anything that seemed *weird.* If I received an impression, I ignored it. If people wanted to talk about psychic abilities, I'd find a reason to physically leave the conversation. I didn't want to know so I blocked my abilities in every way possible. Still, they didn't go away. Now I know that this happened to gently guide me back to my soul's purpose. Time passed and my abilities kept resurfacing until it got to the point that I just gave up and accepted that having intuitive abilities was part of me. They were part of my soul's purpose.

Quite honestly, I just got tired of fighting against what I couldn't seem to stop or control. When I accepted that they were part of me, part of my purpose here, then life started to flow more smoothly. For me, the biggest part of getting past having abilities was releasing the fear of what other people would think about me because I was able to see and know things that they didn't. There was absolutely no way I could find it within me to appreciate my abilities. I just wished they'd go away. I couldn't explain them, but I finally accepted them for what they are and eventually I learned to be thankful for having abilities. It wasn't easy. In fact, oftentimes it was very difficult and it took a long time. Now I know that part of my soul's purpose is to be a teacher. To help others understand how to deal with having abilities. Once I was able to do this, and I finally embraced that part of me and was thankful for having abilities, I found it was easier to be open with others about the things that happened to them and to teach them how to effectively recognize what their abilities were, understand the situations where abilities were presenting themselves and how to develop them if they wanted to do so. Had I not gone through what I did before I accepted my own abilities, had I not fought within myself in order to find my purpose, then I don't think I would be able to teach others like I do today. Now, I am what I believe, which is something I wouldn't have been able to say when I was searching for the reason behind my abilities.

Your soul's purpose is layer upon layer of your true self that is your reason for being. You may be a teacher, a healer, an emotional rock or a giving soul. All of these are part of you. During your search you may work in a variety of jobs and those jobs are helping you to discover what it is within you that you can give of yourself to help others. Think back on your life for a recurring theme. If there is one then it is a key to unlocking your soul's purpose.

Be thankful for the search that has brought you to the place you are now. Appreciate that life is a journey that you will constantly travel. When you connect with your purpose, give thanks for the discovery. Be who you are at your core spiritual being and do what you believe in. Be grateful for all that you are and all that you will continue to grow to be, for in this, you will find true happiness as you connect to the truth of your being. You will become a new you by recognizing the true you.

Be Spiritually Grateful for Your Own Path

Your path in this life is unique. Your purpose for being is special. Sure, you will have shared interests with others in life, but each one of us has our own individual reason for being. Are you thankful for yourself and for the reasons that you're distinctively you?

It is not selfish to be thankful for yourself. Spiritual gratitude is a way to reward your subconscious mind, which is a connection portal to your spiritual essence. Let's look at this concept in more depth for a moment. As human beings, our subconscious mind is also called our conscience, inner voice, higher self or spiritual mind. It is what guides us to do the right things in life and urges us to stop when we are doing wrong things. It is part of our own spiritual self guiding us during our time on Earth. Through our subconscious mind we are able to make connections to the Other Side, to speak with our guides and departed loved ones. Before we are born, we are in our spiritual body and exist with our soul and our subconscious mind. After birth, we still have our soul and subconscious mind, which are the eternal parts of our being that we are never without, but now we also have a physical body and a physical mind that allow us to exist on the earthly plane in order to learn lessons that will allow us spiritual growth so that we may progress to higher spiritual realms.

When you are spiritually grateful for your own individual path, your subconscious mind is nurtured and you are better able to connect to the truth of your divine soul. This allows you to learn the lessons you came here to learn instead of having to repeat them in a future lifetime. By cherishing, nurturing and loving yourself at a soul level, through your subconscious mind, you are being grateful for your life and your own path.

As guardian of your individual path and purpose, you are responsible for learning and achieving what you came here to learn and achieve. You are responsible for your own path, you have free will to improve upon your soul through the earthly experience and the growth or non-growth that your soul creates here is what you'll take with you, on a soul level, when you return Home. If you focus on what you set out to do and are thankful for your path as you learn, then you will encounter a smooth and easy flow to life. It's when you get too caught up in the physical and neglect soul growth that you can walk a difficult path. Now that doesn't mean that you'll never experiences difficulties—you will because some lessons chosen are hard—but it does mean that focusing on soul growth and being thankful for your own path will bring you less hardships than if you're neglecting the soul and focusing on the physical things in life. You can't take material things with you when you die but any growth that you experience on a soul level becomes a permanent, eternal part of you. Spiritual gratitude for your own path allows you to cherish your soul. Nurturing feelings of thankfulness for yourself is like shining a flashlight down a dark path, bringing to light all that is unseen so that you may walk the path in grateful illumination.

As you take a look at yourself do you see a need for change? Are there areas of your life that you could improve upon by changing your attitude or approaching situations in a different manner than your normal approach? If so, then begin by making the changes internally, change your thought patterns first, and then change your actions second. By working within first you're working with your subconscious mind and your soul connection, which will bring about changes in your physical world because of your new thought patterns and beliefs. Adding spiritual gratitude to this change will strengthen any change that you attempt to make. Be sincere in your thanks, sincere in your heart, and sincere in your change and wondrous blessings will result.

As you give thanks for your individual soul path, always remember that you are a spiritual being and the truth of your soul is within you. The more you strengthen your foundation in this lifetime, through responsibility and understanding of your spiritual journey, the closer your connection to your soul. When the connection is close then it's easier to progress in forward motion to attain the goals you've set for yourself in this lifetime.

Spiritual gratitude enhances all that we are and all that we do in each lifetime. When we forget spiritual gratitude, we forget the true nature of ourselves. Every day, be thankful when something nice happens to you. Yesterday, I was pumping gas and was deep in thought because I was worried about our dog that had emergency surgery, had lost her whole litter and couldn't birth the dead pups. After the surgery she stopped eating. I must have looked worried because the man beside me, who I hadn't even noticed, said to me out of the blue "I hope you have a wonderful day today ma'am." I looked at him, smiled, thanked him and wished the same for him. Now that man didn't have to say a word to me. But I was grateful that he did. That small nicety from him seemed to say that everything would be okay. I visited my vet, got a special food for my dog and when I offered it to her, she gobbled it right down.

Remember that spiritual gratitude is about the little things, the niceties in life, as well as the big events. As you begin to live a life full of spiritual gratitude start your morning with a few moments of being thankful for your spiritual path, the people who love and care about you, the accomplishments that you've made and the things that surround you. Then as you move throughout your day, when someone does something nice or unexpected for you, or if you avoid negativity in some way, or any little thing that makes you feel joyful, then take a moment to simply give thanks. The more you practice living in spiritual gratitude, the sooner it will become an ingrained habit, an integral part of your spiritual being.

——3——
Spiritual Gratitude and The Spirit Connection

Spiritual gratitude is a core component of the mind, body and spirit connection. As spiritual beings we are bound by the earthly body but are free in mind and spirit to do anything that we want. When we practice spiritual gratitude by seeking out the sacred and becoming whole, then we can see great transformations taking place within us. Without spiritual gratitude that doesn't happen. We can't help but feel spiritual gratitude because it is a fundamental core part of our beings. As you read through this section, try to think of ways that you can incorporate spiritual gratitude throughout your mind, body and spirit.

Seek Out the Sacred

When you look at the world through eyes of spiritual gratitude, you see it in a different light. One of the ways you can expand your concept of spiritual gratitude is to seek out the sacred. What is sacred to one person may not be scared to another. It is individually unique to every person. If you choose to look at every moment of life as scared, then you alter and broaden your perception and through spiritual gratitude you will be able to see the mind, body and spirit connection within yourself.

Think about what makes your life sacred. The extraordinary is within each of us if we'll only seek it out through the world we live in and within our soul essence. Once you realize what makes your life meaningful and sacred, it will change how you interact with others. When you consider the sacred in your life, it doesn't necessarily have to be religious, although it may be. It can also be spiritual wisdom, the value you place on your life, your connection to the divine and the thankfulness you feel for all that is around and within you. Finding the sacred can be healing and transformative. How do you recognize the sacred moments in your life?

Spiritual gratitude is a key component to finding the sacred in your life. Feeling thankful brings a sense of inner peace and well-being. Taking the time to be grateful causes you to slow down, to give your complete attention to that for which you are grateful, and brings about feelings of wonder and inner peace. You will feel more blessed because you are showing your appreciation and, in that moment, may even feel a sense of separation from the hectic pace of your life and realize a moment of stillness. When you become mindful of these moments, by focusing your attention on them as they occur in real time, you are recognizing the sacred in your life. You have now moved forward spiritually, past the ordinary to noticing the extraordinary, which can bring forth transformation. If you take the time to evoke mindfulness, the more you will notice that for which you're spiritually grateful.

Sometimes you might find it helpful to visit places that others consider sacred to see how you feel in those spaces. There are sacred sites throughout the world; some may even be in your own back yard. There are sacred caves, mountains, springs, trees, bodies of water, rock formations and so on. If you're working on developing you own abilities, visiting the vortexes in Sedona, Arizona is a very popular destination. Wherever you decide to visit, when you're there, you want to make sure you're feeling your own mind, body and spiritual connection to the sacred site. Sometimes the energy in sacred places is very powerful and if you consider the positive energy of its visitors over the years, then that energy can also affect you in a positive manner.

The mind, body, spirit connection that you feel inside when you seek out the sacred can be life altering. It can totally transform your way of thinking and your perception of life in general. You will notice that as you gain a clear understanding of your personal connection to the sacred through the subconscious mind and through spiritual gratitude, you will become more mindful and in becoming more mindful, you become more appreciative. It's a vicious circle—one that will move you forward on your spiritual path. Your spirit becomes one with your subconscious mind and you grow within your true spiritual essence, your spiritual being.

The last part of this connection is your body. As you become clear, balanced and centered in mind and spirit, it is natural for your body to follow. Taking care of your physical self, the body you're living in during your stay on the earthly plane, and being grateful for this body, regardless of looks, colors or defects, will also give you insight to your spiritual essence. Sometimes the body we're given is simply for the purpose of learning a life lesson. Did I ask for red hair? No, but I've learned to appreciate and love my hair (even though it can still be frustrating at times) for the curly red mess that it is, after learning to deal with people who made fun of me for it as a kid. My unruly head of hair made me stand out in a crowd, which I didn't want to do. But the lesson actually goes deeper than just my hair color and texture. Because of my hair, I learned not only to manage negative energy from others regarding my looks (add extremely fair skin and an abundance of freckles and you'll get the picture) but I also learned that standing out from the crowd is part of my life lesson as an intuitive teacher.

As you look for your mind, body, spirit connections to the sacred in your life don't just look forward, but also look back at where you've been and the lessons you've already learned along the way. Remember that the sacred is within you, it is all around you, and it is in every aspect of your life, if you'll only see it that way. If you chose to take a spiritual journey to visit sacred places around the world, then this too can open your mind, body and soul to the sacred. There are many organizations that will plan group retreats at special rates for those who wish to travel together. If this is something that you'd like to do, then search locally for a travel group. It's a wonderful journey to take whether you travel around the world alone or with a group or just sit in your own backyard and see the sacred in your daily routine. Feel spiritual gratitude for all that is sacred to you, for thankfulness is one of the most sacred emotions you'll experience.

Become Whole through Spiritual Gratitude

Being *whole* is something that is often sought after in life. I believe that people seek *wholeness* because they feel the disconnection between their physical being and their spiritual being. In order to find wholeness in life, then you have to look beyond the physical. Living a life filled with mindful thankfulness, overflowing with spiritual gratitude for all that you are and all that surrounds you can give you the whole feeling that you're seeking. People often seek wholeness when they feel something is lacking in their lives, that the things that are missing will in some way make them complete. Sometimes the search can go on and on because the person is looking for someone else to satisfy this need or for a thing to complete them. They are looking outward for wholeness instead of looking within.

Consider that the soul is on a constant quest for perfection in order to move closer to God (or whatever name you give to the Creator of All). In this quest we are struggling with life lessons and deepening our spiritual foundation to become a more mindful, grateful being that is connected mind, body, and spirit with the true essence of our being. That's not an easy thing to do but it is something that we all strive for in our lives, even if we don't realize that's what we're doing. As we journey on our quest, we will recognize at some point that we are beings of energy, of frequency, and that our vibrations are carrying us to higher planes of consciousness as we move forward on our spiritual path. The higher our frequency, the more whole we feel and the more connected to our spiritual selves. The more we learn about our true spiritual nature, the more we feel whole. The more connected we are to nature and the spiritual around us, the more we feel whole. We may never reach perfection, because that's not the goal on this plane of existence, but we can feel whole, with a sense of completeness within ourselves through spiritual gratitude, which is really the foundation and truth of our being. When you view the world through the lens of spiritual gratitude, you are exuding a positivity that will come back to you through the kindness of others, blessings and unexpected gifts.

What are some things that you can physically do in order to feel *whole* in addition to being grateful? Let's take a look at a few ways that you can gain a feeling of wholeness while using spiritual gratitude.

Try to be present in your life every single day. Instead of going through your daily routine by rote, make the most of every opportunity. It's easy to get caught up in the mundane, routine tasks that make up your day and to take things for granted. Being mindful of the blessings in your life allows you to be present in all that you do, to be truly involved in your own life instead of letting the moments pass you by.

Reach out to others. Think less about your own personal wants and needs and more about the needs of others. When you put your desires on the back burner and give someone else your full attention, if you help them when they need help and appreciate them for who they are, what they need and how you can be there for them, and expect nothing in return then you are acting with spiritual gratitude. Not only will this make the other person feel good about themselves but it will make you feel good about yourself too. Some people may desperately need help but will refuse to ask for it. When you help them out of the kindness of your heart, then you are going a step beyond and growing in your own spirituality. In return, you will give them the opportunity to feel spiritual gratitude, even if they don't come right out and say it.

Make changes in your life when you feel a change is needed. Instead of holding back out of fear, take a step into the unknown even if it is difficult. Be thankful for the opportunity to change and grow as a spiritual being. When you think of yourself as fearless, you put aside any feelings that are confining you and preventing you from being brave. When you break out of this mold, a rut that's holding you back, then you can embrace your connection to your spiritual essence. The results might just surprise you.

Be a support system for someone else and allow others to support you. When you give and receive of your emotions you are growing personally and spiritually. It's not enough to let others be there for you if you're not also there for them. Be thankful for the opportunity to share your emotional self with another person and to allow other people to share their emotional self with you. Some of the best friendships are built in this manner. You may just make a lifelong friend in the process.

Smile often—people will wonder why you're happy, or what you're up to, and will usually smile in return. Smiling is one way that you can always show your spiritual gratitude. Have you ever said *thank you* with a frown? If you did, then you probably didn't really mean what you said. Smiling and laughter can open your heart, remove feelings of depression and sadness and make you appreciate the life that you're living.

There are many ways you can feel whole by using your mind, body, spirit connection with others. Talk a walk with someone. You'll exercise your body, clear your mind and share good conversation. Rise above negativity in difficult situations. It may be more difficult to take the high road instead of the low road but it will always be worth it in the end. Work together with others, whether individually or within a group, towards a common goal to gain a sense of belonging.

As you search for wholeness, take control of your life by making changes, being a support system, smiling or doing any other thing that gives challenges you and enables the mind, body spirit connection. Assess the situations you find yourself in and work toward what makes you happy and fulfilled one positive step at a time. Give a lot while asking little in return and you will find that you'll receive much more than you ever could have expected and for that, be grateful.

Transformative Power of Spiritual Gratitude

To transform is to change in form or appearance, to change your nature, character or conditions. You can transform your outward appearance by gaining or losing weight, cutting your hair or letting it grow out, or by changing the style of clothing you wear. You can transform your environment by changing the conditions in which you live, by moving from one place to another or you can change your romantic status by beginning or ending a relationship. A deeper transformation would be if you changed your nature or character by altering your perspective of life.

As humans, we require change when things are no longer working as they have been. When people feel stuck in a routine, you'll often hear them say that they need a change. This is the soul's way to keep us moving forward on our life path in search of finding life lessons and completing them. It may not always be easy to do, but if you truly want a change in your life, or if you don't like the direction that you're headed in, then you have the power within you to make a conscious decision to create the changes you desire and go after them. You can do anything that you set your mind too and spiritual gratitude can help you get there. You will experience many emotions along the way but spiritual gratitude is the one feeling that rises above all else when you need a change in your life. This is when the transformative power of spiritual gratitude becomes very important. It is through the heartfelt appreciation and thanks that overwhelms us as we give ourselves over to the truth of spiritual gratitude at a soul level that allows us to feel the transformation within through thankfulness.

When you experience a spiritual transformation you are changing from within, which affects your actions, beliefs and the way you reaction to situations. A spiritual transformation can be life altering for the long term. It's much more than a short term change like a new haircut or clothing style. Examining yourself allows you to make changes to transform your conscious and subconscious thought processes and be more open to something new. Seeing yourself and your life through the lens of spiritual gratitude alters the way you perceive everything around you. This is especially true if you previously had a negative outlook on life.

If you find that you're constantly looking at the glass as half-empty instead of half-full, or if you feel that situations never go right for you, then this is a sign that you need more spiritual gratitude in your life. Sometimes it's hard to break free from negative thoughts and feelings. Just the nature of negative energy can hold you in its patterns of low level movement, trapping you in the same thought processes and feelings day after day. If you really want to break free from the chains of negative thought patterns, one of the fastest ways to do this is through spiritual gratitude. By giving thanks for the positive things and people in your life you're breaking through the darkness of negativity and illuminating it with light. Spiritual gratitude can push away that which holds you back from thinking in a clear and positive manner. Embrace spiritual gratitude for a life altering transformation in thought and energy.

Exercise: Connect to Spiritual Gratitude

Let's do an exercise that will allow you connect to feelings of spiritual gratitude so that you can feel the transformative energy that is associated with simply giving thanks.

Sit in a comfortable chair or lie down across your bed. You

want to be able to completely relax for this exercise. Feel your body sinking into the chair or mattress until you feel as if you're embraced by the softness of the fabric, you feel warm, secure and safe. Take a moment to think about what spiritual gratitude means to you. As you consider the wondrous gift of spiritual gratitude, think of a time when you were thankful for something that happened to you. Let the feelings associated with this event wash over you, imagine it filling you body, mind and spirit with its positive energy. Imagine it as a flowing blanket of radiance that wraps around you, embracing your spiritual essence. Allow its transformational energy to fill you as you become mindfully aware of your feelings and the real meaning of spiritual gratitude. Once you feel totally immersed in these feelings, allow your awareness to open even more. Now imagine that you are looking up at the night sky and that you can see every single star. Each star represents your actions, words or ever time you've smiled that resulted in someone else feeling spiritual gratitude for you at that moment in time. You may not even realize how many people you have touched during your lifetime until you visualize it as stars. Feel the thankfulness radiating from each of these points of light and allow it to fill you. Know how much you are appreciated just for being you. Hold this feeling close to you and allow it to touch you at a soul level. Once you feel you have a firm grasp and understanding of the good you do in the world and how these feelings of spiritual gratitude can transform your being, then slowly feel yourself reconnecting with the mattress or chair, allow these feelings to flow into your physical body as you reconnect to your surroundings. Open your eyes, smile, and go about your day in thankfulness.

During this exercise you connected to the energy of spiritual gratitude. As it flowed to you from the stars (people) that you've touched during your lifetime, it can also flow from you to touch even more people as you live your life. Spiritual gratitude is a constant moving energy that passes from each of us to the other souls we encounter. It is a living emotion without boundaries or rules. It fills you, overflows and you pass it along to another, it fills them, overflows and they pass it along to someone else. Eventually it will come back to you. Live with spiritual gratitude in your heart and give of it freely.

Exercise: A Conversation with Spiritual Gratitude

Here's another exercise that I'd like for you to do. Take a moment to consider your worth as a human being. What makes you special and worthy of the life you're living? Are you thankful for yourself? Considering your worth might be a hard thing to do especially if you're the kind of person who always thinks of others before themselves.

Spiritual gratitude is part of your foundation as a sacred being; you're naturally wired to be thankful and appreciative. Right now I'd like for you to think of spiritual gratitude as something completely different. If you are a spiritual being made of energy with a vibrational frequency that lives on after the physical body fades, then couldn't spiritual gratitude be the same? In fact, so could love, happiness and any other positive emotion. Negative emotions are to help us learn lessons, so for this exercise, we're not going to think of them as living entities. What if you could have a conversation with Spiritual Gratitude as a living being? What would Spiritual Gratitude discuss with you? What could Spiritual Gratitude teach you? What would Spiritual Gratitude say about your worthiness as a spiritual being on the physical plane of existence?

Since Spiritual Gratitude already resides within you, seeing it as a separate entity can give a greater understanding of the *you* that others see but that you may overlook. Would Spiritual Gratitude say that you are a loving individual? That you are a person who gives freely of themselves while asking little in return? Or maybe Spiritual Gratitude would suggest that you take more time to give thanks for yourself in order to enhance your own spiritual growth. Whatever Spiritual Gratitude tells you, it is all part of your self-worth. Some of it you may have overlooked, other parts of it you may already be aware of in your life.

Now it's time to do the exercise. Grab a notebook so that you can write things down. You'll want to keep this for future reference and so that you don't forget anything. Refer back to this at any time that you're feeling less than worthy. When you're asking these questions go with your first impressions because those will be the most accurate. Don't second guess what you're sensing and feeling because then you may not be giving your self-worth as much value as it actually deserves.

First, think of Spiritual Gratitude as a spiritual being. Is Spiritual gratitude a male or female energy to you? Does it even have a gender? It may or may not. You may see Spiritual Gratitude as a male or female and you might even see details such as clothing, hair color, eye color, height or weight, just as you would if you're seeing another person. Then again, you may only see energy, a moving flow of light or colorful patterns interwoven within it. Spiritual gratitude may appear as a glowing column of light; gold, silver or white. It may be a moving white mist or it could even appear to you as a totem animal. Whatever you see – that is how Spiritual Gratitude is appearing for you and it is right for your soul essence.

Now you're going to ask Spiritual Gratitude some questions. Feel free to use any or all from the following list or to add some of your own. Write down each of the answers as they come to you from Spiritual Gratitude. Remember to answer these as if Spiritual Gratitude is telling you the answers, not that you're answering as yourself. Do this exercise at a time when you're not going to be rushed or interrupted so that you can write (or type) as much information as you receive about each question.

1. Why am I a worthy being?
2. What is special about me?
3. Do you feel that I am generous of myself with others?
4. Do I radiate warmth and love?
5. What do you feel are my five best traits?
6. Am I thankful enough for my own spiritual being?
7. What are the ways that I can become more thankful?
8. What do others feel are my best qualities?
9. How can I move past feelings of sadness?
10. Am I a blessing to others? If so, how?

Once you have written down all of your answers, get up and go get something to drink and take a short break. I want you to separate yourself from the actual exercise for at least a half hour to an hour. Once that time has passed, go back to your answers and read what you've written down. Can you see the value of yourself in a clearer light? Can you see how truly worthy you are to be who you are at this point in time? Can you see how spiritual gratitude plays such an important role in your divine self?

As you work toward becoming more grateful in your life, keep the results of this exercise close at hand. Refer to it often especially if you're feeling unappreciated, are having a bad day or if you simply want to assess your own self worth again. Spiritual gratitude doesn't have to disappear as a spiritual being or only appear in that form for this exercise. If it helps you to be more gratuitous in life, then think of Spiritual Gratitude as a guide that can help you along the way. Seek out Spiritual Gratitude whenever you need to feel a connection to thankfulness and appreciation for yourself and others. By using spiritual gratitude to recognize your own self-worth, you are progressing in forward motion along your own spiritual path. You are a spiritual being full of love, light and spiritual gratitude and that, in and of itself, is an enormous part of your self-worth.

Connecting to Spirit

Do you remember who you are? Deep in the depths of your soul—do you remember yourself as a spiritual being? In this day and age of war, greed, and the chaos of a self-serving society, it seems as if the truth of individual spiritual beings has been forgotten. What would happen if, all at once, everyone suddenly remembered? Things would change in the world almost overnight. Negativity would disappear and love would abound. Arguments, abuse and the depths of despair, which seem to become more and more prevalent with each passing day, would no longer exist if each and every person on this planet reconnected to their true spiritual essence, their core self, their subconscious self that holds all of their spiritual essence. Negativity begets negativity but if, as a spiritual being, you choose to remember your connection to spirit, especially your own spiritual nature, then the world would be full of positive energy.

One of the ways that negativity shows itself in our society is through a general lack of spiritual gratitude. I couldn't tell you how many times that I've encountered people ignoring the spiritual gratitude and kindnesses of others or just being unthankful, with unreal expectations, or they are just mad at the world in general. Just visit any large retailer and you'll see this type of behavior in action. Anger doesn't get you anywhere, neither does ingratitude.

Let's compare these emotions to getting your vehicle stuck in mud. Embracing anger and ingratitude will only have you spinning your spiritual wheels in the mud of negative thinking and unconstructive emotions. The way to move past this is the same as getting out of the mud. Get out a board of thankfulness and wedge it underneath your spiritual wheels to propel yourself from the tainted mud of anger and ingratitude and onto the steady dry land of positivity, happiness and joy. When you do this not only can you free yourself from the mud you're stuck in, but you can also heal any disconnections you may have been feeling within your own soul, heal your interactions with other people and within your world.

Spiritual gratitude is part of each and every one of us and it's up to us to either use it or ignore it in this lifetime. If you're forgotten how to be grateful, then now is a good time to make a conscious effort to remember to give thanks and watch as positive things flow to you. Think of the Law of Attraction which says that what you put forth to the Universe will come back to you. If you're putting out negative thoughts and emotions then you'll receive negative events in your life in return but if you're putting out positive thoughts and emotions then you'll receive positive experiences in return. Adding thankfulness to the concepts of the Law of Attraction brings tremendous results. When you reconnect to your own spirit, then you'll notice that the flow of your life feels much smoother because you're now connected to your true spiritual being. By realizing the power of your emotions, especially spiritual gratitude and love, you create the reality that you live in and are connecting to your own Universal Truth. Once you realize this connection between the spiritual self and the physical self, then you really can reach any goal that you wish to attain in this lifetime. Reconnecting to your spiritual self can help undo any negative thought patterns that you have taken as your own due to misconceptions in the world. You know your own truth and should always follow that truth instead of following what society dictates especially if it is in direct opposition to how you feel. Feelings of spiritual gratitude should always come from the heart and of your own free will with spontaneity and joy instead of being something you are told to do but that you don't really mean.

Exercise: Connect to Your Spirit

Emotion is a powerful tool that you can use not only to see your spiritual self but to see and connect to the spirit within others. For this exercise you're going to realize just how powerful your emotions are when you're connected to your spiritual self through the physical self.

Find a mirror that you can walk by repeatedly, not simply stand in front of it (like you might find in a bathroom). Now, walk by and glance at yourself. What do you see? Did you see your physical self? Do it again. What do you see? Your physical self again? Each time you walk by the mirror try to look deeper. Glance into your own eyes as you pass by. When you see your spiritual self instead of just the physical body you're in then stop at take a good look deep into your eyes. There you are! Now say "I love my spiritual self!" and mean it. You can also try saying this to yourself in the morning, something like "Good morning spiritual self! I love you!" By connecting to your spiritual self in this way, you will feel powerful emotions and a strong sense of self-worth because you are seeing the real you that resides within the physical body.

You can connect to others in the same way by really seeing them as the spiritual being that they are deep within the physical body that they're occupying. Seeing another in this way allows the divine to shine through.

You can take the first step now by embracing spiritual gratitude and connecting to your spiritual self. The resulting feelings of peace, joy and happiness will make you wonder why you waited to make changes in your life. Consider the things that you normally take for granted and be grateful for them. If you can't think of something then consider the fact that you woke up this morning. Give thanks for another wonderful day on this Earth. Things may not always go smoothly but you're here to experience them.

As you connect to your spiritual self, you'll probably notice that you'll also connect to other spiritual beings such as your guides. When you're able to feel the truth of your spiritual self, it opens the door to meeting and understanding those who remained on the spiritual plane to help guide you during this lifetime. You will probably feel the spiritual gratitude that your guides have for you because you are now more mindful of the thankfulness at the foundation of your being. Being mindful opens the eyes and heart to receiving feelings of spiritual gratitude from others whether they reside on the physical earthly realm or in the spiritual realm. Take the time to learn from this connection to the divine and your guides. They can teach you many things if you'll only take the time to listen and learn. Remember to express your sincerest spiritual gratitude to those who help you along the way both on Earth and in spirit form. The opportunity to experience this plane of existence is one that you can be thankful for because one day, you'll be back on the other side guiding others during their journey here. The foundation of spiritual gratitude will benefit you in more ways than you can ever imagine if you will only embrace it from the heart.

Recognize the Support You Receive

We do not go through life alone. Some people are born into families who love and support one another while others may experience a more difficult family life. I've heard it said that we can't help what kind of family we're born into, but I believe that we choose our families prior to being born and have agreements with them so that we can learn as much as possible during our time on the earthly plane. If things are difficult in your family, take a step back and look at the lessons before you. You might not be able to change your situation right now but you can learn from it. Each person has friends, mentors and is interconnected to thousands of people during their lifetime. Some of these people are in your life for the duration while others come and go. Some may appear multiple times; as in the cases where you lose touch with someone and then reconnect later in life. Regardless of the circumstances surrounding our interactions with family and friends, you will learn from one another along the way. The lessons may not be easy ones but you can chose to be spiritually grateful for the lesson itself.

There are many times when you can express spiritual gratitude for the support you receive along the way. A meaningful thank you when someone holds a door open for you may not seem like much in the way of thanks but if your arms were full and it would have been a struggle to open that door on your own, and you're extremely grateful for the help, then that thank you came from your heart. You may have experienced the kindness of strangers many times in your life. In fact, showing kindness to others is something that many people do in order to pay it forward in their lives. By showing kindness to others, that kindness is returned to them in the future.

Being spiritually grateful for the people that you come into contact with not only show others how you feel about them but it also positively influences you on a soul level. When you can be spiritually thankful you are growing and moving forward on your own sacred pathway by sharing your divine light of spiritual gratitude with those you meet along the way.

During times when you turn down someone's help, you can still show your appreciation for their offer to help you, even though you prefer to go it alone. There are some challenges that we need to figure out by ourselves in order to experience the growth they bring. Just remember that in the overall picture, none of us could succeed alone in the physical world without the assistance of the other spiritual entities existing on both the physical and spiritual planes. It is a difficult journey and that is why it is in our nature to be helpful to those around us. We should make it a habit to be spiritually grateful for the help of others because their assistance will make the experience joyful and easier than if we try to go through life keeping to ourselves and distancing ourselves from others who are on the same path.

As spiritual entities, we are forever learning and moving forward to become a better spiritual being. Our guides in this lifetime are usually entities that are in our circle of souls on the other side. They may be entities that we've known since the beginning of time or a new friend. Their position isn't to tell you what to do or to make your decisions for you, but instead to offer their advice so that you can make the decision yourself. Thus the reason we call them our spirit guides. They often have a clearer vision because they aren't encumbered with the physical realm.

Be willing to give of yourself by helping others in their time of need or anytime you want to do something nice for them. You don't have to have a reason to be feel spiritual gratitude for another person; you can appreciate them just as they are right now in this very moment. Let them know how you feel.

—4—
Spiritual Gratitude in Action

Through awareness you can find a reason to be spiritually thankful every day by taking a moment to stop what you're doing and look at situations from a clear point of view by listening to what other people are *really* saying. It's so easy to speed along on the "I'm too busy" train and watch the world pass by through plate glass windows. If you can get off that train or find a way to slow it down so that life is no longer a blur passing you by, then you can find more joy in your life through spiritual gratitude. It's hard to find ways to slow down and make spiritual gratitude an important part of your life in today's fast paced society. But if you can find reasons to be thankful, then it's easier to maintain a steady pace.

Remember to Act with Spiritual gratitude

As a writer, people often ask me where I get the ideas for my books or what kind of research I do in order to write them. Just like every other author, I research for my books by reading and investigating and if it sounds right to me, including my feelings on that information in my book and listing the research book in the bibliography. However, you might have noticed that the bibliographies in my books are usually very short. That's because I write about things I know and feel that are part of me and that come from my heart. I get my ideas just like every other writer does, from my experiences, from a remark that spurs an idea or a discussion that turns into a *what if* session and ends with, "Oh my gosh – that's a great scene for a novel!" or "I really should write about this in my next nonfiction book." I also get my ideas by being mindfully aware of the world around me. I notice the little things (sometimes a bit too much) by being a careful observer. This section came from such observations.

The other day I was in one of the big retail chain stores when I got in the checkout line behind a couple. A few minutes later a kid said "excuse me" and went by me to be with his family. He had a box of cookies in his hand. The man turned, saw the cookies and went ballistic. He started screaming and yelling at the kid, who hadn't even asked if he could have them yet, yanked the kid by me and out into the aisle to make him put them back, yelling all the while. When they came back, the child looked absolutely miserable. There was another box of the same cookies on the shelf by the candies and the kid just kept looking at them longingly. The man was barking orders at him the whole time they checked out and basically treating him poorly while the lady ignored the whole thing. This type of situation happens all across the world—I've seen it myself numerous times and not only with children but with adults and elderly people.

That experience led me to this section because what I saw didn't have to happen that way. We wouldn't treat other people badly if we remembered that spiritual gratitude is part of our core foundation. When we act from within our foundation and in spiritual gratitude, then we see the world and the people in it differently. All that had to happen in this situation was to say, "We can't buy cookies today but maybe we can get them next time." The problem stems from a lack of remembrance. We've forgotten the kindness in our hearts and to be thankful for all that is—even the children.

When we are genuine in our spiritual gratitude, then the positive energy of our thankfulness flows from us to all of those around us. When you're living in spiritual gratitude it's impossible to be unkind because it's just not part of your being. You are filled with an exceptional amount of gratefulness for those around you and you send this energy to them. They receive it and feel joy from your positivity. In this instance, had the man handled the situation with gratitude, then the child wouldn't have been embarrassed and upset. He would have been given the opportunity to learn to act with kindness instead of acting in anger. So when you're faced with an instance where your patience is being tried, just take a moment to breathe, visualize yourself at your soul's center and feel the spiritual gratitude within you. Then, act from this place of positivity instead of the negativity of anger or frustration. Everyone around you, including yourself, will be much happier.

Have you ever heard that saying that *what goes around comes around?* Spiritual gratitude works in the same way. What you put out into the Universe comes back to you. The more positivity and grateful feelings you give to others, the more it will come back to you in the form of blessings and good situations in your life. In the process, the spiritual gratitude that you give helps other people along the way as it's making its way back to you.

While prevalent in the world today, harboring feelings of unkindness, criticism and judging others isn't the way our souls are made. Negative situations experienced on the physical plane have pulled us in instead of allowing us to feel the positive energy that is flowing in our core being, just waiting to be released.

Now don't get me wrong—there are many people that have

embraced their soul essence and are living lives filled with spiritual gratitude. Right now I'm talking to those of you who may have forgotten or lost your connection to your true spiritual natures. Once you remember that you are a gratuitous being, then you will begin to see that any challenges that come your way aren't reasons to jump into the waters of negativity and bad behavior but are simply obstacles to overcome so that you can grow in your own spirituality and positivity. It is our responsibility to accept these lessons and challenges as gifts and to really appreciate what they are teaching us.

It is also important to know that not everyone will choose to remember their soul essence and act with spiritual gratitude. Some people will choose to live in negativity, unbalance and without opening their eyes to the truths around them. That is part of their own life lessons—to move past the lower energy patterns into the higher frequencies of their own soul connection—and hopefully, when the time is right, they will be able to do this. Not everyone does and in those cases, the lesson will be repeated in a future lifetime. The important thing is to not let those who choose to live this way make a negative impact on your own growth as a spiritual being.

If you choose to remember and choose to act with spiritual gratitude from your heart in all that you do, then you are being mindful of the good in situations, and you're able to see and feel the blessings associated with heartfelt spiritual gratitude. This is a lesson for you—to take the time to stop, look and listen to your surroundings and to move forward towards happiness, joy and the new you that spiritual gratitude can create. Living your life with appreciative purpose, with positive feelings of joy, and through mindful awareness can bring more blessings than you could ever think possible. At times it may be difficult to stay on the path but if you wander off the trail, then spiritual gratitude can put you back on track. You are a blessing to the world. Let everyone experience your shining light.

Take Time to Share

As a child you were probably taught to share your toys with other children so that you didn't appear greedy or selfish. Sharing is hard for kids because it means they have to wait to play with something that they're enjoying right now. Sharing is more than just letting someone else borrow your possessions. Sharing is an important lesson in understanding another person's feelings and in learning to wait your turn.

As adults, each of us participates in sharing and waiting our turn every day. If you drive a car, you share the road with other drivers and you must wait your turn at stop signs. You can't just barrel through them out of turn or you run the risk of not only getting a ticket but of causing a car wreck. We also have to wait in lines at the grocery store, the post office and numerous other places but we can also share smiles, conversation and our positivity with others who are also waiting. You never know how that brief moment that you share with someone who you'll probably never see again will affect you (or them) so it's always fun to make it an engaging experience.

Sharing is a normal part of life but it is also a choice. When you share, you give of yourself through kindness and unselfishness. Sharing is when you are generous, helpful and loving to another person. You can show others your caring nature by sharing kind words and thoughts or by generous actions. You can share any number of things like your knowledge, beliefs or innermost thoughts. You can share food, conversation, gifts or your time. In fact, you can share just about everything in life. If you're married, in a relationship, have children or friends—then you have chosen to share your life and yourself with these other people. You can share in small ways or big ways. Something as simple as opening a door for someone is sharing the kindness of your soul with them. Listening to a friend or helping your neighbor with a project is sharing of your time and of yourself. Giving your possessions to someone in need or buying things for others, even if they didn't ask for them, is sharing. You can choose to share at any day or time, not just on special occasions or holidays. Sometimes sharing is appreciated more when it's not expected.

We can also choose not to share. There are some days when it's difficult to share, days when you just want to be alone with yourself and that's okay. These are excellent times to share within yourself through spiritual gratitude. Exactly what does that mean? It means taking the time to give thanks for you. Maybe you could make a list of the reasons that you feel grateful for yourself. Or if you're feeling blue, write down the reasons you're out of sorts and then try to come up with a counter reason that you can give thanks for. For example, if your job has you down, you can be thankful that you have a job to annoy you. Look at the reasons you're upset with work and then look for the positive in those reasons.

When you share your spiritual gratitude with others you are giving your thankfulness in an open and honest way. You're giving of yourself in the moment with spontaneity and through love. A little bit of spiritual gratitude can go a long way in helping yourself and those around you. If you're in a bad mood, it can be changed to good cheer in a matter of moments when you're thankful. This happens because instead of looking at the negative, you've changed your perspective to the positive simply by being appreciative. And this appreciation transfers to others. Maybe someone else is down in the dumps or having a bad day, but your spiritual gratitude towards them lifts their spirits and they in turn become thankful and show their spiritual gratitude to someone else. Just like a smile is contagious, so is spiritual gratitude.

Think about the times that someone else has shown you spiritual gratitude. When someone else appreciated something that you did, how did you feel? Were you happy because you were noticed and appreciated? Did you feel more willing to do more or to go out of your way to do something nice because of these feelings of spiritual gratitude? This often happens in the work environment. You're much more willing to do an even better job than you normally do when you know that the work you're doing is appreciated. When you feel overlooked or taken for granted or overworked and underappreciated, then it makes going to your job a chore instead of something to look forward to with joy.

The family environment is the same way. Each member of a family contributes to the overall energy dynamics in some way. In our family there is our techno guy, our fix it guy and our comedian, the cool big brother and the keeping it all together dad and me, the jack of all trades. Each one of us contributes part of our character, love and spiritual gratitude for one another each and every day. Take a few moments to consider the integral workings of your family unit and how spiritual gratitude for one another plays a part in each day. Do you see any places where more spiritual gratitude needs to be shown? Are you overlooking something? If so, then share your spiritual gratitude in more than one way to those closest to you.

Taking the time to be grateful and sharing your spiritual gratitude with others will make a positive impact on your life.

Sharing your joy, laughter, fun times, quiet times, conversation and meals together will open the door to closeness to and appreciation for the people who you may sometimes take for granted. Being mindfully aware of each person that is close to you and appreciating the unique qualities that makes them who they are is a great place to start. Sharing your spiritual gratitude with others is part of your spiritual essence and it will be rewarded with blessings that come back to you. Share your spiritual gratitude with someone else today.

Forgiveness and Spiritual Gratitude

Forgiveness through spiritual gratitude is powerful. When you are able to forgive others for past wrongs by being thankful for that person, regardless of any bad things they may have done to you, then you are rising above negative emotions and are showing appreciation for their role in your life, even if it was a difficult situation. If it is hard for you to be thankful, especially if, as a child, you were forced by a parent or guardian to show gratitude for things when you really didn't feel grateful for them, then it can be difficult to get to a place of thankfulness. Forced appreciation can close you off from reconnecting to the spiritual gratitude in your soul but you can heal these feelings through forgiveness. On a soul level, each of us understands the life lessons that we have chosen to learn. We know that each of us will participate in these lessons for the greater good of our own soul or to help another entity on their path. If you feel that something needs to be forgiven, then you must forgive to feel right within your own spiritual essence. How do you do this?

Exercise: Forgiveness

There are a couple of ways that you can offer forgiveness through spiritual gratitude. If you're not in contact with the person who wronged you anymore, it will still benefit you to forgive them, heal the hurt within you that they caused and move forward on your own spiritual path even if you can't offer your forgiveness in person. When you forgive them, you'll feel like a weight has been lifted from you. You'll feel free of the negative emotions that you've been clinging to in the past.

Get out a notebook or paper. At the top of the page write down the person's name that did something to you that you haven't forgiven. Write a paragraph about what happened. In another paragraph write how you felt about the situation.

Now, look at what you've written and see if you can find a reason why they may have acted in the manner that they did. Can you find one? Really think about the situation from their point of view. Did they even realize that they were hurting you? Did you say anything to them at the time? Do they know how you felt then and how you feel now? Write your thoughts down in a third paragraph. Now in the last paragraph, write down your feelings of forgiveness. List the reasons why you're forgiving them and the result that you'll feel once you've forgiven them for their actions or words.

Another way you can forgive someone is to connect with them face-to-face if you're still in contact with the person. Let them know that their actions hurt you and that you've forgiven them for the past hurt and their previous actions. This can be very difficult to do and if you don't feel ready to take such a big step, then include them in your list so that you can forgive them within yourself and move past the event. If you're out of contact with the person, but you really feel that you must forgive them in person, then see if you can find them online through social media. If you can, then reconnect with them and clear the air. The result may be that a misunderstanding is cleared up and the relationship is back on solid ground. Taking that first step can be difficult but know that you're doing this to heal yourself through spiritual gratitude, even if the other person isn't willing to do the same.

When you forgive someone you're giving them your love and are feeling thankful for them instead of holding onto feelings of anger or betrayal. By replacing the negative feelings with positive ones you're moving closer to your soul essence and true spiritual being. It takes courage to open your heart again after you've been emotionally hurt. But doing so can make you feel lighter and more at peace within yourself. This is an important aspect of spiritual growth which can be achieved through experiencing spiritual gratitude.

Forgiving Yourself

One of the hardest things to do is to forgive yourself. If you were involved in a situation where you were in the wrong, then the first thing to do is to recognize your part in the situation and admit that what you did or said was wrong. Forgive yourself for your actions and then, if possible, ask for forgiveness from the other person. It may be given to you and then again, it may not be. If it's not, then understand that the other person is not at a place on their own spiritual path where they can freely forgive past hurts. We all move at different paces on our divine paths and you can only be responsible for your own actions. If you're not forgiven, you may feel hurt and angry that you tried to resolve the situation and couldn't. But you know what? That's okay. At least you tried. No one ever said forgiveness through spiritual gratitude would be easy—often life's most difficult lessons are the ones that propel you along your spiritual path the fastest. Through your effort, you can feel the spiritual gratitude associated with forgiveness or with asking to be forgiven and move forward. The result will be that you will feel a sense of release from the negative emotions associated with holding on to these past hurts.

Forgiving yourself is important. The surrounding situation doesn't hold as much weight as the fact that you need to be at peace within yourself. You'll find this peace when you give yourself permission to be thankful for the experience, own that you were in the wrong, and then forgive yourself for your part it the situation. It doesn't matter if anyone else gives their forgiveness to you as long as you give it to yourself. If you don't forgive yourself for something that weighs on your mind then it will become regret, holding you back from reaching your fullest potential. When you're able to forgive yourself, you release the negativity surrounding the situation and allow yourself to feel more enthusiastic about your life and grateful for the blessings that you receive. This in turn brings joy, peace and happiness to you.

When it comes to forgiving and being forgiven, it can sometimes be very difficult to do because you can't force your feelings. You have to be ready to forgive someone before it can happen inside of you and that's something that only you will know when you're ready to do. However, don't make it more difficult than it has to be. Sometimes we can be our own worst enemy. You can *what if* or *if only* the situation to death, or we can wish things were different and avoid the truth but that's not going to change what happened. It is what it is and you just have to accept that there isn't anything you can do to change the past. The other person may have been in the wrong or you might have been in the wrong. All you can do is forgive or ask for forgiveness and learn from your mistakes. If forgiveness isn't given you have to be willing to accept that and forgive yourself for your part, if necessary, and move on in spiritual gratitude and with joy in your heart.

Fill Your Expectations with Spiritual Gratitude

Expectations are actions and events that you are looking forward to or that you anticipate happening. When you expect something, you regard it as highly likely to happen. If you fill your expectations with spiritual gratitude, then you can ensure that even if what you expect doesn't happen, you can still experience thankfulness.

Spiritual gratitude, thankfulness that stems from the depths of your soul, can give you an inner feeling of powerful calmness in all aspects of your life. If you expect the unexpected, and live like you are dying, and if you do this by filling all of your expectations with spiritual gratitude, then you can feel at peace within, regardless of the outcome.

This was a hard lesson for me. I had been disappointed so many times in life that I just gave up on expecting anything. If I didn't have expectations, then I wouldn't be disappointed, right? Well….it took me a long time to see it, but that's not exactly true. Even if you're not expecting something or even if you don't expect people to act in specific ways, you can still be disappointed in something that didn't happen, someone who acted incorrectly or you can be disappointed in yourself. Expectations don't mean that you'll never have disappointments. Expectations filled with spiritual gratitude will allow you to be thankful for the possibilities instead of disappointed. It's a good switch to make in your point of view but it's not an easy one. My attitude now is one of *let's just wait and see what happens* before jumping the gun and making plans that might not come to fruition. I no longer back my feelings about expectations—it's fun to feel excited about something that might happen—but I also try to feel thankfulness for the possibilities instead of disappointment if the thing I'm expecting doesn't happen.

If you connect with your true spiritual nature it is much easier to fill your expectations with gratitude then if you take a materialistic point of view. The key is to look beyond the physical to the spiritual to gain clarity of vision in your expectations.

When you aren't living in spiritual gratitude you may feel life isn't fair, you may place blame for your circumstances or relationships on another person, you might feel your life should be different and someone else needs to change it for you. You may take life for granted and flow from one bad situation to another. You can change all of this and alter your expectations by being genuine and sincere, and by beginning to look at your life with spiritual gratitude, thankfulness and joy. Doing so allows you become mindfully aware of all of the good things in your life beyond your material possessions. Instead of always wanting more and more things and the next greatest gadget, you begin to be thankful for what you already have instead of constantly wanting more. Now, there's nothing wrong with wanting new stuff if it's not the *only* thing you're focused on in your life and a driving force within you. When you realize you must take responsibility for the situations you're in, and those situations came about through your own actions, and when you learn that only you can be responsible for your own spiritual growth and the lessons you chose to learn, then you're growing in spiritual gratitude. In essence, you become more enlightened through spiritual gratitude. It's amazing how looking at life in this manner can truly wake us up to more possibilities and expectations that we ever dreamed possible. Living a life filled with spiritual gratitude is already a part of your soul being, part of your foundation, and once you embrace it as such you'll feel its positivity throughout your being.

If you're not experiencing your expectations through spiritual gratitude, then you may have created unrealistic standards in your mind of those around you or events that you expect to happen. This was one of the problems I had and why I often felt disappointment—I expected more than the person could actually give and then I'd be disappointed that they hadn't delivered. That was unrealistic of me. Once I began looking at my expectations of others with spiritual gratitude, I realized that my previous high levels of expectations for other people had pretty much gone away. Instead of expecting anything, I began to just accept people as they are and enjoyed being in the moment with them instead of expecting specific actions from them. I looked at them with spiritual gratitude instead of expectation. That was a hard lesson for a girl in her 20's but it is a lesson that I'm glad I learned early in life. I still have expectations—for example, I expect my kids to do well in school—but I only ask them to do the best that they can do. If they don't make straight A's, I'm not going to freak out over it. As long as they are doing their best, that's all I can ask of them. And really, that's all you can ask of anyone in any situation—to give it their best. So, think about it for a moment; are your expectations of others unrealistic?

As you view your expectations through the eyes of spiritual

gratitude you will experience more happiness and joy. When you're grateful, positivity flows to you, washing away any negativity that you may feel. When you release your hold on expectations, especially unrealistic ones, you can focus on yourself and your own spiritual growth, instead of worrying about what someone else is doing (or not doing) to live up to what you expect from them.

Be grateful for everyone and everything in your life. Expect little and you'll receive a lot. The ebb and flow of life, as we connect to our truth within, will enable you to understand that spiritual gratitude and unrealistic expectations are at opposite ends of your emotional spectrum. When you're filled with one, you can't be filled with the other. Choose spiritual gratitude for positive well-being.

Embrace Life, Live with Intent from the Soul

When you live in spiritual gratitude, you also live with intention because it keeps you focused on the many blessings in your life instead of any problems that may arise. Spiritual gratitude helps to keep everything in perspective so that you don't make mountains out of molehills or let minor problems get you down. It's finding the silver lining in bad situations and viewing circumstances from a positive point of view.

A few months ago as I brought my dog inside the house, I reached back to get the leash and a strong wind chose just that moment to slam the door shut, knocking my hand back about a foot before crushing my finger at the nail bed. I have a very high tolerance for pain but this unexpected accident had me crying for about a half hour. It hurt so much I couldn't put ice on it or even run cold water over it. It took three months to heal and grow out a new nail. When it happened I told one of my friends about it and she said, "At least you didn't cut off the end of your finger!" And she was exactly right. I'd been thinking negatively because I had hurt myself but after she said that I started to think about what would have happened if the end of my finger had been cut off. I would have been extremely delayed in finishing this book, I would have been in much more pain, I would have ended up at the hospital and well…you get the picture. It would have been much worse than just a smashed finger. When you look at a situation with spiritual gratitude, and what you're thankful for that *didn't* happen, it helps you to embrace what *did* happen and deal with it with thankfulness. I know I'm very glad that I still have my whole finger and purposefully began thinking of the situation with positive intention after being reminded.

Living with intent is one of the most powerful things you can do when you remember to do it (which is why you have to make a habit). I discuss this in my book, *365 Ways to Raise Your Frequency*, and I'd like to give you a quote from that book right now.

"Intention is the biggest factor in controlling frequency. I'm going to say that again because it's very important: **Intention—your reasons for doing what you do, acting the way you act, and treating people the way you treat them—is the biggest and most powerful way to control and elevate your frequency.** Every intention carries a vibration with it, and that vibration can immensely affect your overall life."

When you live in intention, you will raise your frequency. If you add spiritual gratitude to the mix, then you're truly living the best life you can live and are embracing the life you've been given by living with intent from your soul. Living with intention and in thankfulness gives us strength, hope and the knowledge that whatever you face in this world, you'll be able to move through it in spiritual gratitude and love. In times of trouble, just remember that *this too shall pass* and difficult times don't last forever. For example, my finger did heal in time and the situation passed. Your soul knows this, even if you forget. Look at your intentions in everything you do. Are they true to your soul's essence or have they become skewed by the challenges of living in the physical world. If they have, and only you will know if your intentions are of the purest good or if they've become tainted, then use spiritual gratitude to examine your intent and make changes in your approach. When you're living in pure honesty and though spiritual gratitude in your intentions then you will truly embrace life and live it in happiness and joy.

Intention is powerful as is spiritual gratitude. The combination of the two together can take you from feeling like a victim to feeling in control of your life. You can see the greater plan for your existence by looking past this physical realm to the connection to your soul essence. You can see gratefulness all around you and appreciate more in life then you can by walking blindly in ingratitude. Spiritual gratitude combined with an awareness of your own intentions can be life altering, enlightening and can awaken you to your soul's purpose.

Exercise: Take Stock of Your Intentions

In order to examine your truest intentions, there are a few things you need to think about. For this exercise I want you to just think about the following questions. You can also write them down if you'd like.

- Do you do things to truly help others or do you do them for what you think you can get out of it;
- Are you giving from the heart or out of a sense of obligation,
- Do you volunteer because you really want to help or because it makes you look good in the eyes of people you want to impress?
- Do you present your true nature to the world or do you hide behind a mask of fake intent?
- Can you think of some unique ways that you can apply feelings of thankful for the things you intend? (For example if you intend to be a giving person today, would bringing a surprise gift of coffee and donuts to your co-workers show how much you appreciate them?)
- Does the intention need to change from a negative outlook to a positive one? If so, write down exactly what you can do to make the change and why you'd be grateful once you've accomplished the change.

Think about these questions as you examine your intentions. These starter questions will probably lead you to ask yourself additional personal questions about your true intentions. Let those questions come naturally through this exercise and examine them as well for further enlightenment.

Make sure that your answers are pure and without ulterior motives. Try not to hide the truth within yourself instead of writing it down. Be honest with yourself and write down honest answers. Once you've gotten it all written down, you can always refer back to it at a later date to reconnect to your feelings about your intentions or to see if your feelings have changed.

Once you see the truth of your intentions and you apply the

thankfulness of spiritual gratitude to them then you can change your point of view and your actions. Making these changes will allow you to embrace all that life has to offer while passing the positivity created within yourself to everyone you encounter.

Did you find it difficult to examine your intentions and let spiritual gratitude fill your heart while doing this exercise? If so, it might be a good time to start a daily spiritual gratitude journal if you haven't done so already.

Create a Journal, Make a List, Board, or Chart

I'm a big fan of lists. They keep me organized and on schedule. Every year when I buy the kid's school supplies I purchase a student weekly/monthly calendar that looks like a spiral bound notebook and runs from July of one year to June of the next. I use it to keep daily, weekly and monthly list of things that I need to do. I have a tiny version that I keep in my purse to jot down things as I think of them and later I transfer them to the notebook calendar. And I never throw these away. It's fun to look back at them from time to time to remind myself of where I've been and what I've done in life. I can see times that I was extremely busy and other times when I was moving at a slower pace.

You can use this same philosophy and organizational style when you're working on becoming more thankful in your life. You can also use a journal if you prefer blank pages over a calendar format. If you do choose a journal, either choose one that already has dates at the top or take the time to date each page before using the journal for the first time. This way you'll be aware if you miss a day.

There are a few different approaches you can take to using

your spiritual gratitude calendar or journal.

- The first approach is to write down the things you're grateful for as you progress through your day. If you're grateful for a lot of things, you will find that you're making entries quite often, which can be time consuming. This is a good approach to take when you're getting into the habit of making thankfulness an integral part of your life because it makes you mindful and more aware.
- You can also make a note above your daily *to-do* list of one thing to be grateful for that day. You'll see it each time you check something off of your list and can take a moment right then to feel appreciation for that one thing.
- Another approach is to write down a list of several things that you want to give thanks for during your day. You can use this list as a reminder by looking at it several times a day and taking a few minutes to feel spiritual gratitude for the things you've written down.
- You can use your spiritual gratitude journal is to make a list of things you want to feel spiritual gratitude for a week in advance. Make each item on the list unique each day and then use the journal as a daily reminder. By planning out things that you want to give thanks for, you can avoid repeats during the week. That said, being grateful for things more than once is completely fine. You can also add to your planned list during the day based on the events you experience.
- Another way to use your spiritual gratitude calendar or journal is to write down the situations you experience, whether they're positive or negative, and then write down why you're grateful for that situation and any lessons you

may have learned from it. By writing down a more detailed recount of the experience, it will be as if you're experiencing it all over again (even if you look back on it many years later) and you can give thanks for it again at that time.

Boards and charts are other excellent tools to use to become more mindful of what you're grateful for in your life. Similar to a manifestation board (where you paste pictures of the things you want to draw to you on it), for your gratitude board you'll paste pictures of the things in your life you're grateful for. Then hang the board in a place that you'll see it often. This may be near your work station or in your bedroom, or in any room of your home that you frequent. Then, when you glance at it, take a few moments to give thanks for the things on your board. You can change the items on the board or have several different boards placed in various locations throughout your home. It is a tool that serves as a visual reminder to be spiritually grateful.

If you work on the computer a lot you might also create a slideshow of pictures of the things or people that you're grateful for and then let them rotate on your desktop. You can even create your own pictures with whatever photo editing software that came with your computer and place only text inside a box with a variety of different background colors to give thanks for something very specific. Save them as jpegs and include them in your slideshow.

Charts can be used in the same manner. You can make a chart of what you're thankful for and refer to it or you can use a chart to log how often you're giving thanks. This chart can be simple or as complex as you want to make it. You might graph that you were thankful for ten things today and eight things yesterday or you may log how many times you stopped during your day to give thanks. If you want to get really detailed, you can log each of the different things you were thankful for and chart how many times you appreciate each of those items. Charts are an excellent tool to use especially when you're starting on the journey of making thankfulness a habit in your daily life.

Lists, boards and charts may be something that you use daily, weekly or monthly to keep a record of the things you're thankful for in your life. When you look back on these tools, you may notice how your spiritual gratitude has changed over time. You may notice times when you're more thankful and other times when you're less mindful of your thankfulness. By noticing the flow of your practices you can make changes and become more thankful and living in spiritual gratitude over time.

If you're the type of person who dislikes keeping a journal or making lists or if you don't have the time to keep a journal then simply give thanks throughout your day, each and every day, and remain consistent in this practice.

—5—
Slow It Down to Simplify Your Life

We move through our daily routines at a warp speed that would make space travelers proud. In order to truly savor and appreciate within the depths of our soul, we have to slow down. We have to make the time to smell the coffee, roses or whatever favorite thing you enjoy smelling. Life isn't a race to see who can do the most before it's over. Instead it's a journey where we learn from one another as we discover more about the spiritual side of ourselves. When you slow down you'll realize there is more to be grateful for than you may have thought and you'll see clearly that which you should release.

Consider resentments. Is there anything in your life that you've resented for a long time? Maybe the way a significant other treated you and now that past situation still affects current relationships because you can't let it go? You know what you have to do, right? You have to let it go. Am I oversimplifying this? Yes. Because sometimes, we put so much drama onto ourselves and work ourselves into a whirlwind of turmoil which makes it very difficult to see a situation clearly. When your heart is involved, when emotions are at a high point, when the situation hurts so bad all you can do is cry—it's extremely difficult to step back and see it clearly, past the emotions, because it's easier to stay in the turmoil. Stepping back means you're starting to let go and sometimes the root problem is that we don't want to let go, we don't want to leave the problem or person behind because we're connected to it. I know you can't drop everything instantly, turn your back and walk away. If you're experiencing a deep pain then the issue is going to be much more complex for you but you can start to let go by taking baby steps and releasing resentments, forgiving the past and moving into the future. Just because one person acted badly doesn't mean that everyone will.

When you're analyzing your past, spiritual essence, talents, gifts, abilities and beliefs so that you can fully love yourself, great things can happen. Not only can you become more aware of any hurts that you can forgive or heal within yourself but you will also be able to consider possibilities that may never before been presented to you. Loving yourself is all about accepting each and every part of yourself and boosting your self-esteem through thankfulness. When you love yourself, you'll find it easier release the old negative feelings, the resentments from the past and give each new person you meet a chance to connect to you without reservation.

Be Spiritually Grateful for the Small Things

You have the ability to make a total transformation within yourself if that's what you truly desire. It's as easy as getting back to the truth of your soul, appreciating all that comes your way and being mindfully aware of the world and people around you. Spiritual gratitude is an emotion filled with positivity but it also goes deeper because it allows a connection between your heart and soul. You'll often affect others with your spiritual gratitude and they'll in turn affect someone else. It's like passing a smile around. You just can't help but smile back when someone smiles at you.

Spirituality has, at its core, a foundation of spiritual gratitude as does self-improvement. In general, when we are thankful not only are we more spiritual aware but we're able to change ourselves, and improve upon our beings on the spiritual, emotional and physical levels. We may become more helpful; have better relationships, experience less stress and more spiritual well-being. We have a renewed sense of self-worth and our self-esteem soars. We live with a calm peace of mind and are a positive influence on others. And we get to this point by being naturally and spiritually grateful for the little things.

As you begin to develop a deeper sense of spiritual gratitude, you may begin with feeling thankfulness for the big things in life like your health, the people you love, your job, home, car or other material possessions. These are great places to start, but to truly develop a spiritual sense of spiritual gratitude you have to go deeper and develop your feelings of spiritual gratitude so that they are naturally a core part of your being—spiritual gratitude is part of your spiritual foundation already—and by making it a *conscious* part of yourself it will always help you regardless of any other thing that is happening in your life.

So now you are grateful for the big, important things in life. That's fantastic! Let's look at the small things. When you become mindfully aware of the little things in your life it is easier to make spiritual gratitude part of your core essence. Let me give you an example of when I was thankful for the little things in life.

When you're driving a vehicle you'll often see people texting, eating, putting on makeup and doing any number of things in their cars. Personally I like to put on alternative music and sing and seat dance which drives my kids bonkers because they're embarrassed that "someone will see you, Mom!" I think it's funny because I could care less if anyone sees me or what they'll think if they do notice me. I'm happy and I'm enjoying my favorite song and most people don't notice other people anyway. After my finger got slammed in the door, I wasn't able to sleep much because it was throbbing all night, so I felt exhausted the next day and my finger still hurt and well, I wasn't in the best of moods so I just kept to myself and didn't say much. Later that day, we were in the car when I noticed one of my kids fiddling with the radio. The next thing I knew my favorite song, the one I always seat dance too, was blaring out of the speakers. I looked at my kid and he just grinned. Wow. He'd put that song on because he knew that I wasn't in the best of moods and wanted to make me feel better. I was so grateful for having such a wonderful, caring son in that moment. I didn't feel like it but I forced myself to sing and seat dance to that song because he'd gone to the effort to play it for me in the car and in that moment he didn't care if anyone saw me singing and dancing, and you know what? I felt immensely better afterwards! It was a little thing to do, but it meant the world to me because it was done in gratitude.

Exercise: Finding the Little Things

There are many little things that you can be thankful for. A hummingbird sipping nectar from the flower in your garden; the lady at the store who held the door open for you when you could have just as easily opened it yourself; the rich smell of (insert favorite food here) drifting in the air; the smell of a fresh summer rain; the two-year-old kid who smiles at you in a check-out line and says hi; the guy at the intersection that let you go first; the glass that didn't break when it fell in the sink; stumping your toe and it didn't hurt too badly; the soft nicker of a horse greeting you; a sunrise and a sunset; a nap; a surprise phone call; a cool rock you found while walking; a hug; puppies; kittens; a smile; taking the right turn when you thought you were lost; the wind; the warmth of the sun against your face; laughter.

As you're going through your day, slow things down—you don't have to go through life at the speed of sound, you'll miss too much. Be mindful of the little things that you can feel spiritual gratitude for and then speak words of thankfulness out loud to remind yourself of the simple things in life for which you're grateful. This gives you an understanding of how wonderfully fantastic it is to be alive regardless of the challenges you face along the way.

For this exercise, I want you to get out your camera. If you don't have one, you can buy a disposable one at a retail store. They even have digital disposable cameras now. Pull out a camera and start taking pictures of the little things that you're grateful for and then put those pictures in a book or in a file on your computer so you can look at them often. Noticing and appreciating the simple things in life can open your mind and heart to a new world.

Let Go of What No Longer Belongs in Your Life

Clutter, clutter everywhere. It can just sneak up on you. One day your house is clean and the next day it just seems to be a cluttered mess. How did that happen? If you're hanging on to things that you don't need, it can happen quickly. Junk mail is the biggest culprit in our house. For some reason it just seems to accumulate instead of being thrown out daily. When you feel your surroundings are getting too cluttered and congested, start throwing things away. If there are items that are worthy of being donated, then give them away. When you get rid of clutter in your environment, you free the energy to flow as it should instead of being caught up behind the clutter.

What does this have to do with spiritual gratitude? Even though it takes time to do, you should be thankful for clutter because it acts as a catalyst to make you move. It gets you going so that you can release the things that no longer belong in your home or office environment. When you clear it out the energy flow can return to its normal positive patterns. Once you complete the task, your home or office is free and clear of the things that no longer belong there.

Let's take a look at your personal life. Sometimes we have to clear our personal situations just as we would clear our physical environment. Are there people in your life who are self-serving and who really don't have your best interest at heart? People who are difficult or have a negative outlook on life? People who want to bring you into their drama? What would your life be like without them in it? Would you have less stress and feel lighter in spirit? Would you be happier? If you answered yes to these questions, then now might be a good time to make some changes when it comes to your relationships. Only you can decide if this is true for you and it's advisable to take a good, long look at these relationships before taking any action. Don't rush into a decision you might regret later. If you're unsure, try limiting your time with the person in question and then see how you feel. We all go through times when we are involved with someone who only wants to be around us because of *what we can do for them*. If allowing that person a place in your life isn't serving *you* any longer then maybe it's time to move on.

On the flip side of this, if someone no longer wants to be a part of your life, then let them go. Don't try to hold onto them when they don't want to be held on to. If they feel the need to leave, then there is a reason behind their decision and, in the grand scheme of things, they're not part of your long term life plan. Some people come into our lives to help us learn a lesson and then they leave—it's a short term stint, not a long term commitment. It's easier to accept the flow of people in and out of your life if you accept the fact some of them are only short-term guests. That doesn't mean you won't reconnect with them in the future. You might meet them again but then again you might not. Enjoy and appreciate each person while they're part of your life and release them if they want to move on without you. Sometimes it's really difficult, especially if you're romantically involved, but if you can find it within you to release them when they want to go, it will be better for you in the long run.

We can *let go* in every aspect of our lives. What about things that you do? Are you working too much? Do you have enough time for yourself or do you have so much on your plate that you never seem to slow down? In this society it's easy to get overwhelmed by all of the things we're expected to do. If you're in a family where you're carrying the majority of the weight, then try delegating responsibilities to other members of your family. They'll be grateful that you taught them responsibility instead of depending on someone else to do everything for them. I know that I often tend to take on too much work and then I feel like I never get to take a break. I've got ten things going at once and it can get quite demanding on my time and draining to my energy. When I notice that I've gotten into a situation like this, I look at the things that I do and if I realize that I'm no longer enjoying something, I stop doing it. If it's making me happy, if I feel that I'm accomplishing something positive by the work I'm doing, then I continue, but if not, then it's already served its purpose in my life and it's time to let it go. I will also take breaks from doing readings and book cover designs when my plate is too full and resume them at a later date when my calendar isn't so full.

Now take a look at your emotions. If you're carrying around a lot of emotional baggage, if you're holding onto past hurts, if you're trying to help someone who doesn't even try to help themselves, these types of situations can leave you feeling upset, depressed or stressed out. If that's the case then you should really try to release them. Emotional baggage can get quite heavy and if you're having a hard time releasing it, you might stop trying and fall into negative thinking. By releasing emotions that are doing this to you and replacing them with feelings of spiritual gratitude for the situation, even if it didn't happen according to your plans, then you're letting go. This is a positive action that will be rewarded with new positive emotions.

Letting go through spiritual gratitude allows you to free up space spiritually, emotionally, and physically and open space is very inviting to new positivity. Creating new space by clearing out the old will allow new things to come to you. The connection to your soul essence increases when the energy is flowing freely between your physical self and spiritual self. When your hands are full to overflowing it's difficult to grab new opportunities when they present themselves. When you let go of things which no longer belong in your life then you are accepting and preparing for the good things that are on their way to you. Be grateful for them and when they arrive, grab them with both hands and give thanks that you've been given a new chance to shine.

Only What You Need

As you're letting go of what no longer serves you simply hold on to only what you need on a physical and spiritual level. I'm not talking about stripping yourself of all worldly possessions, although you may even find yourself donating your excesses to charities or businesses that help others by distributing your donations. Instead, I want you to consider what it is that you truly need in life because sometimes, less is more, and when you have too much you can start taking the good things for granted and become less grateful. Take note of what really makes you happy. If it brings you joy, then you need it in your life. When you consider only what you need then you will feel more spiritual gratitude for the things that you already have. You'll be less inclined to be wasteful because you're focusing on only what you need. This is a way to simplify your life through spiritual gratitude and mindfulness.

Sometimes you can't always have the physical things that make you happy but if you're able to hold onto them in your heart, then you're still thinking of them with spiritual gratitude. For example, I love horses. I've loved horses since I was big enough to know what a horse was. As a kid my dad built shelves for my room that I could sit all of my horse statues on them. I've lost count of how many I had but I'd save up my money to buy them and then put them on display in my room. I read every horse book written and dreamed of the day I could have my own horse or pony. When that day came, I spent every minute I could with her. The years passed and she passed away and I eventually went away to school and sold her foal to a kid that lived nearby. Life was taking me in a direction that wouldn't include horses for many years. My love for them never diminished, I just wasn't in a position to own them again until 2006. Since we've owned horses I've felt like I've come home within myself again. Like the part of me that's still the little girl who grew up on the farm with her ponies had been jumpstarted again. There's just something about a horse that is calming and makes me feel at peace inside. While my husband and I currently plan to always own horses, life could take me in a different direction again and if it does, horses will remain in my heart forever. We never really know what's in store for us but for the moment, I'm living my childhood dream again and I give thanks every day that I'm able to have horses back in my life. Right now we have a black stallion just like the one in the books I read as a child. For me, he's a dream come true.

Being aware of the things that make you happy deep down on a soul level will help you choose only what you need in life. You can discover what makes you happy by taking the time to sit down and make a list of the things that make you smile, things that you enjoy doing or experiencing and that gives you a feeling of joy. Even if you can't have that physical thing, you can keep the concept of it alive in your heart, making it an internal part of you, as I did with horses in the past and will probably have to do again someday when I'm old and feeble. When you're aware of the things that make you feel happy, you're not blindly ignoring what brings you joy. If you listen to your own inner guidance, then what you want in life is really only what you need instead of extravagance. For me, having a horse in my life feels important on a soul level, a part of me, but to someone else, a horse may bring feelings of fear or they may think of it as a luxury that they don't want. Someone else might hate the smell of horses while I love their unique scent. When you think of only what you need, those needs will be completely different for everyone.

You can use the *only what you need* philosophy in other ways to. Do you need a bank loan? Ask for only what you need. How about at the grocery store? Buy only what you need. If you're in a drought area, use only the amount of water that you need. The *only what you need* philosophy means that you're not wasting things that might also be needed by another person. If you have extra and don't need it, consider giving it away to someone else. For them, your excess might be exactly what they need.

Spiritually, you will discover your own truths as you need to know them. Have you heard the saying that when the student is ready that the teacher will appear? You don't have to worry about being overwhelmed with spiritual concepts as you're learning to connect to your soul essence because you'll only be given what you need to know when you need to know it. Overwhelming a student with too much information doesn't give them the time they need to grasp and understand the concepts. Your spiritual guides want you to understand what they're trying to teach you. They want you to integrate Universal Laws and Spiritual Concepts into your own spiritual beliefs. They don't want you to throw their teachings aside because you're overwhelmed; therefore, they give you only what you need to know at a specific point in time. This helps you to move in a forward direction, with positivity and thankfulness for the knowledge given, instead of back pedaling in overwhelming frustration. That's why learning about our own spirituality in a lifelong event.

Sometimes we really need to face our past in order to move into our future. If you have issues that are dragging you down, or blocking your forward movement, then you have to address those issues in gratitude. If you've been ignoring them, thinking that they'll go away, well, that's not going to happen. They'll sit back there in your mind, festering away and causing negativity in your life until you've no choice but to address them. Go ahead and get them out of the way by looking at them with spiritual gratitude. Think of the things you really need in life and hold onto those things in your heart if you can't hold onto them physically. Know that you'll only ever want what you need and in those needs you can find peace and happiness.

Follow Your Dreams

Each and every one of us can follow our dreams. No dream is too big or too small. You can realize every dream you have if you continually strive for it. Spiritual gratitude is important in reaching for your dreams. When you're thankful for what you desire, it makes it easier to achieve. Being true to yourself and thankful for your ideals is important in reaching for your dreams. Do what you love and live your dream.

One of my favorite sayings is, "Can't never could do anything." I don't remember where I first heard that saying (probably from my mom) but it stuck with me. Every time I hear someone say "I can't" I always respond with that saying. If I start thinking that I can't do something, then I say it to myself. You can do anything if you'll only try. Let me tell you a personal story that shows exactly what I mean.

We own Friesians. They're very big horses. While I had one in training I decided to take a few riding lessons just to get back into practice since it had been a while since I'd ridden. Well, the horse I was going to take the lesson on was huge, much bigger than my Friesian mare that was 16.2 hands. He was nearly 18 hands (that's 72" or six feet at the withers) and round as a barrel. The first words out of my mouth were "I can't ride him! He's too big!" Well, long story short, after complaining about his size and fighting the fear of falling off (because I *was* out of practice and that's a *long* way down) I finally climbed (yes, climbed!) up there, with the aid of a huge mounting block, and you know what? He was the best horse ever! I rode him for several weeks and he helped me get my seat back. That wouldn't have happened if I'd given up at that first "I can't". I was extremely thankful for that horse's nature and willing attitude.

What is your dream? Usually our dreams are something that we would love to do, something that will make us happy while we're doing it. If you keep your dreams in sight, remain thankful for them along the way, and keep pushing forward in your attempt to reach that goal, then you will realize your dreams. Your dreams are going to be unique to you and might make you stand out from the crowd. That's good because you're being who you are at a soul level, and if you're living your dream you're doing what you love. It will be fun, even if it's work, because it's what you love doing. I've always heard to do what you love because it will make life so much easier. And that's true. What if you hate going into work every day? Then you're not doing what you love. It might be time to start considering a different career. When you're passionate about what you do, and give thanks for being able to do what you love, then you'll be successful at it and make a living at it. You might experience a few bumps along the way as you're striving to achieve your dream, but that happens to everyone.

Living your dream doesn't mean living someone else's dream for you. Sometimes that can happen. There are plenty of cases of parents who didn't achieve their own dreams and try to make them happen through their children's lives. That's not really fair is it? Wouldn't it be better to let the child reach for their own dream? Instead of living your dreams through someone else, make a stance and go after what you want to do. It's never too late and you're never too old. Let's say you love a particular sport but due to some injury you were unable to continue playing. Instead of living your dream through someone else that can play the sport, get involved in some other way. Be a coach, or organizer or any other position you can do that will enable you to continue to be involved in the sport you love. You'll feel better about yourself and will be living a version of your dream. You might not be playing but you're still involved, which still counts. Be thankful you're still able to participate in some way and do what you love. If you have the opportunity to do something you love, but chose not to because of fear or feelings that you *can't* do it, then you may end up with regrets in life. Let spiritual gratitude be the main ingredient, give thanks for the opportunity and then fulfill your desire for it by following through and accepting the gift of living your dream.

Walking your individual path and living your dream may seem hard at first. You may be afraid to do it and those first few steps are the hardest. I wanted riding lessons so I'd be ready to ride my horse when she was trained but standing on my tiptoes to saddle up that giant horse wasn't easy. I was afraid to get up on his back. It was hard and honestly, I was scared. But once my butt was firmly in that saddle and the reins in my hands, all of that melted away because I was doing what I dreamed of doing. I needed to practice in order to ride my own horse, which was green and not very used to having a rider on her. In order to ride her, I had to get better though practice. It was all worthwhile the day I sat on my own horse and rode her around the arena.

Whatever your dream is, you *can* do it. If someone tries to squash your dreams, don't listen to them. You'll face naysayers who may not want to see you succeed and will criticize you, say your dream is stupid, or others who may feel fearful that you'll be disappointed if you don't reach your dreams or you'll hurt yourself trying to achieve them. Ignore the naysayers and their criticisms and be thankful for the people who care enough to voice those fears, even if they don't come out nicely, and keep moving forward towards your dream. You are responsible for your own happiness in life and knowing that, how could you do anything other than reach for your dreams?

Remember, can't never could do anything—but you can!

Live in Love and Spiritual Gratitude

Love and spiritual gratitude are, to me, the two most important emotions that we, as humans, are able to feel. Everything we do should come from a place of love and we should maintain spiritual gratitude as a core foundation of our being. Could you imagine a world without love and thankfulness in it? I could, but I really don't want to. It would be a sad, sad place.

It's a fact that we aren't always grateful. When you're living in the moment of life, it's easy to forget to be thankful, especially if someone hurts you emotionally or when things or going wrong. As you make spiritual gratitude a habit in your life, living in love will help strengthen your foundation so it's easier to remember to be thankful. When your heart is full of love it's difficult for negative emotions to be part of your spiritual essence. But even then, it can happen. It's part of being human and living on the physical plane of existence.

I'm a very down-to-earth person. I try to see life as it is and not through rose tinted glasses. I try to accept people as they are, and not make them into something I want them to be. I wasn't always this way but it's something I learned along my own spiritual path. I'm thankful I learned these two lessons:

- Life will throw you unwanted curve balls no matter how spiritually centered you are and what matters most is the way you deal with them.
- You cannot change anyone; they can only change themselves when they truly desire a different way of being.

Let's take a look at each of these for a moment.

Curve Balls: Are you looking at your life through rose colored glasses, ignoring things that you don't want to deal with and hoping they'll just go away? When life throws you a curve ball, how do you react? Do you get frustrated, upset and angry? Do you rant and complain? Sometimes it's good to feel these emotions briefly at the onset—it's natural—but don't languish in these feelings. Feel them, and move past them with as little drama as possible so that you can begin to see the situation in a clear light. Try to hold ranting and complaining to a minimum so that you don't say something you'll regret later. Think about what you can do to resolve the situation and how you can handle it so that you can once again feel spiritual balance. There's no doubt that when life's curve balls hit you, they can throw you completely out of balance and into a tailspin, but you don't have to *completely* spin out of control. When you're living in love and spiritual gratitude it's easier to dodge that curve ball or, when it hits, quickly turn, grab it and throw it back to the Universe's pitcher. It's all in how you see things. If your perspective is one of love, and you're thankful for all that life has to offer, even the challenges, then you'll have an easier time dealing with things than someone who isn't living in love and spiritual gratitude.

Changing Others: Would you want someone to change you?

Would you even *allow* it? If not, then why would you try to change someone else? Change only comes when a person wants to live in a way that is different from how they currently live. It happens when the person has an experience that alters their beliefs or makes them see things in a new light. It has to come from within them. Living a life full of love will allow you to understand that, as much as you want someone to act in a certain way, you can't force them to do it. In fact, when you try to force what you want upon someone else, you'll usually get the opposite result from what you're trying to achieve. Instead of trying to force change, appreciate them as they are—faults and all. If they are going to change it will happen as it's supposed to happen, when they're ready, and often it takes that person living in love and spiritual gratitude to make a change within their spiritual selves. There are just some things that we have to do alone. Spiritual, internal change or any kind of personal, emotional or physical alterations to our beings are part of our individual journeys, not something others can force us to do.

Living in love and spiritual gratitude means feeling these emotions for everything in your life; it is making them an integral part of your being. When you do this you'll notice that you take less for granted because you're looking at everything differently. When good things happen to you unexpectedly, when you're surprised by the loving kindness and spiritual gratitude of others, then you will feel incredible spiritual gratitude in return simply because you weren't expecting what you received.

You can do the same thing too. There are so many people in the world who need help in some way. Do you have time to volunteer at a facility that cares for people? If so, that's fantastic but if not, do you have time to speak a kind word to someone you meet during your day? Or can you pick up the box that an elderly person dropped in the store? Buy someone a meal? Spend time with someone who is lonely? There are many big and little ways that we can share love and spiritual gratitude with others and all of them are just as important.

Think about your family for a moment. Is the balance of chores equal or is one person doing more than another? Is everyone appreciated equally or has everyone gotten so content with one person doing the majority of the work around the house that the person is unintentionally taken for granted? Think about what would happen if that person wasn't around to do everything. You'd have to do it yourself, right? The overworked person might be Mom, Dad, one of the kids or anyone else in the household. If you realize that someone is doing more than they should, or more than is really fair, then pitch in and help out. The overworked person will sincerely appreciate it and you'll feel spiritual gratitude because you were able to do something to help someone you love.

Living a life full of love and gratitude that comes from deep within your spiritual being, your true essence, is one of the greatest things you can do for yourself.

—6—
Change Your Attitude to Open Your Heart

If you ready to transform your life you can do it by opening your heart and mind to spiritual gratitude. Simply giving thanks will help you change your attitude and approach to how you live. You might think that such a simple act as feeling appreciation for someone or something in your life couldn't possibly bring about such grand results. I'm here to tell you that it can. Thankfulness, appreciation, kindness and spiritual gratitude are all names for the same feeling. It's how you apply that feeling in your life and how your actions and reactions arouse the same feeling in others that will show you how spiritual gratitude connects with your spirit. Transformation is waiting for you if you'll only give spiritual gratitude an important place in your life. Let's do an exercise that will help you release negative feelings.

Sense of Entitlement

What does life owe you? Nothing—absolutely nothing! There are many people in the world who will agree with this statement but there are also people who feel a sense of entitlement that will disagree. For those who are living with a sense of entitlement, they may feel that life or other people owe them something instead of feeling that they will receive back in life what they put into it. They may have a superiority complex, or feel that rules do not apply to them. They may think they deserve special privileges that others don't have or that they should be treated in special ways, just because that's what they *feel* they deserve. They may want to receive perks and other things that they've done nothing to earn.

In this life, no person owes another person anything unless it is a physical object that has been borrowed. If you borrow money, then yes, you owe that money back to the person or financial institution that lent it to you, but you're not owed a good job, a car, a vacation or a home just because you feel entitled to it. These are all material possessions that you have to work hard for and earn in your life.

If you have a sense of entitlement you may also feel that God or the Universe owes you simply because you exist. You may feel anger and resentment because you didn't receive what you felt you deserved. Was this thing you deserved something that you should have worked for in order to receive it? If it was and you didn't do the work then you really can't feel angry about that now can you? Here's the thing—if you really want to make a transformation in your life then it can't always be *me, me, me* but instead it has to be about other people. Changing your attitude by opening your heart to possibilities, instead of thinking about yourself all of the time and then looking at these possibilities with spiritual gratitude can bring about a complete transformation for you at a soul level.

Now, not everyone has an overinflated sense of entitlement as I have just described. Many of us may feel entitled only once in a while and about little things—but it is still a sense of entitlement. So, examine yourself and see if you are hanging onto feelings that others owe you something or that you deserve something *just because*. When you are used to getting everything you want immediately, then delay getting those things. When you have to wait for something you appreciate it more. Releasing any feelings of entitlement goes a long way in reconnecting to your true soul essence and the truth within you.

When you live with a sense of entitlement you may feel angry and resentful or easily frustrated more often than you feel happiness and joy. The problem with feeling entitled is that it has negative effects on you and those around you. It can make you feel like you're being cheated by life, or that the thing you feel entitled to has been stolen from you. But this really isn't the case at all—it's just the way you're feeling by holding onto a sense of entitlement. These viewpoints are created in your own mind and are often a result of being disconnected from your true spiritual nature. Once you're able to reconnect to your spiritual side, and who you are at a soul level then transformation is inevitable.

To transform from feeling entitled, look at the good things in your life though spiritual gratitude as blessings and gifts. When you give thanks for the things that you receive instead of being angry because you didn't receive more than what you got or something different that you wanted, then you can begin to appreciate more and feel entitled less. If you've been living with a sense of entitlement for a long time, this can be a hard habit to break. And it's exactly that—a habit that you've formed in your mind. All habits can be broken if you want it badly enough. Releasing feelings of entitlement can be very rewarding and can cause tremendous growth on a personal and spiritual level. Expressing feelings of thankfulness for the good in your life is the easiest way to begin to release the negativity associated with feeling entitled.

It's also about seeing life clearly instead of selfishly. Think about this: in life, do we deserve to have people treat us with respect, with fairness and equality? You might have answered yes to that question, but I promise it's not a trick question. I just want you to think about it for a minute. In life, everyone wants to be treated with respect, fairness and to be equal to everyone else but that doesn't mean that you *are entitled to* being treated this way. If you are treated in this manner it is because the people who treat you this way are doing so out of the goodness of their heart, because they want to treat you in this manner, not because you deserve it. It is a gift from others to you. That's the difference in spiritual gratitude and entitlement. Spiritual gratitude comes from the heart and entitlement comes from a wrongly placed feeling that others owe you something. Spiritual gratitude is part of our core foundation and usually comes naturally to the majority of people. We want to do what is right, we want to be loved and we want to treat people fairly because we want to be treated that way in return.

If you've seen something of yourself in this segment, then it's probably a good time to examine your beliefs and your approach to life. Are you connected to your soul essence? Do you understand your life's purpose? Do you look at life with a sense of thankfulness and positivity? If not, use spiritual gratitude to change your perspective, your actions and the way you interact with others. Going through life with a sense of entitlement can hold you back from receiving the blessings that you can gain through spiritual gratitude. By recognizing feelings of entitlement, stopping those feelings, and then replacing them with spiritual gratitude, you can completely transform yourself within and without, which allows you to live with a heart full of love and a sense of peace and contentment.

Release Resentment

Resentment is described as feeling or showing displeasure at a person, act or remark resulting in a sense of injury or insult. Resentment is an emotion that can block you from feeling spiritual gratitude and appreciation in your life and it severely lowers your frequency (personal vibration). It is one of the most negative emotions because when you're filled with resentment, you're also filled with ill will towards another person who you believe has wronged you, whether that belief stems from a real event or one that you have imagined. This ill will can be a slight feeling of indignation or a hostile, evil feeling of rage if you look at both ends of the resentment spectrum.

Guess where resentment comes from? Unfulfilled expectations or a sense of entitlement. If you expect someone to do, act or be something and that doesn't happen, or if you expect someone to give you something and then they don't, you can harbor resentment because you didn't get what you expected from that other person. If you feel that you deserve something because you're entitled to it but then you don't receive it then you can be left with feelings of resentment.

We've all experienced feelings of resentment at one time or another in our lives. Think of something that you've felt resentment over. Sometimes a person can be so consumed by feelings of being wronged that they overlook the fact that what they've really been given is a gift. Think of the person who cares for an elderly parent, who becomes part of a blended family or who cares for a sick person. In each of these cases the person could feel resentment because of the duties they have to perform that may be difficult. But if they look at the situation as a gift then they'll see if differently. Didn't that elderly parent care for you when you were young because they loved you? Doesn't being part of a blended family involve loving the people in that family? And caring for someone who is sick—well, you do that because you love them, right? Then love and spiritual gratitude are the gifts you're given and are giving in these examples. Sure it can be very difficult at times but spiritual gratitude and love flows between the two of you. When the person changes their perspective and realizes the gifts in their life, then the feelings of resentment can change almost instantly to feelings of spiritual gratitude.

Let me give you an example. When I was growing up one of my chores was to milk the cow twice a day. Most days I didn't mind but other days I resented having to get up early and go out into the cold weather to milk that cow before school. Then one day someone said to me that if I didn't milk her, her udder would explode. I was raised on a farm and knew that udders didn't explode, but it made me think about my chore from the cow's perspective. What if I didn't milk her? Would her udder get so tight that it hurt? Was it a relief to get all of that heavy milk out when I milked her? Was that cow thankful that I milked her twice a day since she no longer had a calf to nurse her? Once I looked at my chore from her perspective, I lost my resentment about it. Now, at my current age, I can look back and see that milking that cow was a gift because I learned how to take care of a large animal and I wasn't afraid of it. I never thought I'd use that skill again, but several years ago one of our horses got mastitis when her foal was weaned and guess what? I had to milk that horse until the infection cleared up. I'm thankful for all of those cold mornings because it taught be a bigger lesson than just milking a cow. It taught me to care for an animal that relied on me every day.

We can shift our viewpoint and release any unrealistic

expectations that cause resentment by looking at the situations with spiritual gratitude instead. Once examined and released, there is no longer a need to feel resentment because you have resolved the issue within your own mind, body and soul. You'll no longer flow in currents of negativity but will now break free and swim in a stream of positivity. This transformation will raise your frequency, allow you to see the world in a new light, and fill you with feelings of thankfulness.

Resentment cannot survive if spiritual gratitude is present in your life. When you hold onto resentment, you're keeping the negative feelings you may have experienced alive in your heart in the form of self-pity, bitterness, anger, envy, self-righteousness, hatred, jealousy and any other negative emotion that can be named. Holding onto resentment and these negative emotions is like an infection festering in your body. I know, this might sound gross but it's what resentment does to you. As your resentment is held inside, it grows, just like an infection, until one day it has to break free. Just as your body will eventually slow down due to the illness until you get antibiotics, resentment can cause you to blow your lid so that all of the anger and frustration you feel can escape unless it is treated with spiritual gratitude. You can't hold all of those negative emotions in forever. It's unhealthy both spiritually and physically. Why would you want to be miserable by going over and over negative things in your mind, when you could be happy in spiritual gratitude?

Don't make yourself sick with resentment. If you do, you'll be unable to participate in all that life has to offer. Resentment can make you withdraw from people and from enjoying many experiences in life. Living life apart from others, simply because you are resentful, is negative. Release resentment and allow spiritual gratitude to fill your heart with joy. Open your heart, change your attitude and transform your being through spiritual gratitude.

Exercise: Shed Negative Feelings

I'm often asked how to shed negative feelings, or how to turn negatives into positives. Negativity can hold you back when you're trying to become more spiritually grateful. Consider this when you're thinking of spiritual gratitude and negativity: oil and water don't mix. I want you to think of any negative feelings you have as oil and your spiritual gratitude as water. Now, using creative visualization, imagine filling a clear glass with the water of your spiritual gratitude and then letting your negative feelings float on top like oil. Take an imaginary spoon and stir as hard as you can, mixing the two together. As the mixture separates and the negativity floats back to the top of your thankfulness, pay particular attention to the flow of energy within you. Feel the negative emotions floating upwards toward the top of your head, filling your head and upper body. Once the negative oil particles rise to the top of the glass, imagine picking it up and pouring off the negative oil. As you do this, also imagine your crown chakra at the top of your head opening at the same time and as you pour out the negative oil, the negativity held within you also releases out of your body through your crown chakra. If you want to feel more grounded, you can also reverse this and imagine the negative energy filling your legs and then flowing out of the soles of your feet and into the ground. Once you have sloughed off all of the negative energy you can now focus on the positives in your life—all of that water of spiritual gratitude that still fills your glass and your being. Examine what you feel and write down your first impressions of those feeling. Be thankful for all of the things you find inside when you observe these positives. Use this exercise anytime you need to get back on track with spiritual gratitude.

No One Knows Everything

No one knows everything, but everyone knows something. When we share our knowledge with others, we are giving of ourselves. Sharing our knowledge with a dose of humility, allows us to be gracious in our sharing and not boastful. When we encounter questions to which we don't know the answers, there is absolutely nothing wrong with saying, "I don't know." As humans, we're not expected to know everything, but instead we're constantly learning and bettering ourselves through knowledge and experiences. In learning, we can be thankful for the knowledge of others, so that they may teach us, whether it's how to use a power saw or how to connect to our inner selves. There is a plethora of things that we can learn in our lifetimes if we'll only seek out knowledge and appreciate the teachers of that knowledge.

Have you ever encountered people who feel they already know it all and have nothing else to learn in life? These people will teach us patience and will help us to understand how interesting other people can be when they're not shoving their *extreme wealth of knowledge* down your throat. Instead of becoming annoyed with this type of person and avoiding them, we should be grateful for what a know-it-all can teach us.

Oftentimes a person who thinks they know everything has a negative outlook on life. It may be internal and difficult to notice or it may be show itself very well. They may often come across as critical, condescending, and uncaring simply because they don't listen to the opinions of others. They may constantly interrupt to bring the conversation back to themselves, criticize others, never ask about the other person in the conversation and act as if only their opinion has value. This type of person can make it difficult for you to feel spiritual gratitude for them because they ignore what you say, put down your opinion or turn it around and make your opinion their own. They usually don't even realize that they may very well be hurting your feelings with their rude behavior and incessant talking. If you say you've done something, they've done it too, only better than you did it. If you say that you want something, they already have the latest most advance version available, it doesn't matter what you say, they'll top it. And please, don't ever say that they're wrong or a rampage may start.

Being around a person who thinks they know everything can be very frustrating. It makes you want to avoid them at all costs simply because you feel as if you can't be yourself around them and that everything you say is going to be put down. It's difficult, especially if the person who knows everything also happens to be someone you love. The person may be insecure or hasn't learned to be humble and coming across as if they know everything makes them feel important and pumps up their ego. If we look at the person who thinks they know it all as someone who is insecure or who was never taught social skills, then it's easier to feel spiritual gratitude for them. It doesn't mean you have to condone their behavior, but you can be thankful for them as they are.

How can you show more spiritual gratitude to a person who acts like this? Well, it's not easy when it's difficult to get a word into what is often a one sided conversation, but it can be done. It's important to try to look at the world from their point of view. Can you step into their shoes for a while? When people come across as know-it-alls, maybe a little patience is needed. Or maybe you have to be a little firmer with them in order to participate in the conversation. I've told people that I know who are like this to "hold that thought for a minute and consider this", which is something I normally wouldn't say. But it grabs their attention for a moment and gives you the opportunity to add to the discussion.

If you're a person who acts like this how can you present yourself as less of a know-it-all and more of a knowledgeable person? Through spiritual gratitude. When you appreciate that the person you're talking to is a spiritual being just like yourself, a being who has feelings and opinions that may be different from your own, and you're thankful for the time that they're spending with you, then you look at them in a different manner. They're no longer someone you're talking at but become someone you're talking with. Instead of only voicing your own opinion, spiritual gratitude allows you to feel comfortable within your own skin and to give them the opportunity to share their ideals, thoughts and experiences with you. If you feel insecure in any way, then take the time to face those insecurities and know that people will like you for whom you are especially if you don't try to force your ideas on them or belittle them if their opinions differ from your own. When you look at life through the eyes of spiritual gratitude the world looks brighter, calmer and filled with joy. By letting go of a know-it-all attitude and embracing spiritual gratitude, it can make all the difference in the world when it comes to relationships with others. It's worth a try and you might be surprised at the positive results.

It is impossible for any one person to know everything. It's better to appreciate one another and take the time to get to know others. There are so many opportunities to learn from every person that you meet and from those you have known your whole lifetime. Sometimes it's perfectly fine to put the knowledge you've already gained in your back pocket and absorb all new information. Doing this allows you to add to your knowledge bank and becoming a richer person overall. Spiritual gratitude can help you if you'll open your heart and mind to your true spiritual essence and welcome the new opportunities that are presented to you.

Don't Compare Yourself with Anyone Else

Each person on this planet is a unique spiritual and physical being. There aren't any two of us that are exactly alike. Even if you're an identical twin, you're still two different people on the inside. We all have different motivations, different dreams and different pasts, all of which makes us the unique individuals that we are.

Comparing yourself to another person can sometimes cause you to belittle yourself because you feel you're not as good as the other person or as worthy. Don't do this to yourself because it will only make you upset. Comparisons are great if you're launching a new product and are trying to determine the best marketing strategies, but they're lousy if you're comparing your life or your looks to someone else because you'll only make yourself feel less than what you really are. When you compare yourself to someone else, it might go something like this: "I wish I looked like her" or "I wish I had his fashion sense" or "I wish I had his/her curly hair."

Tell me this—what does it accomplish to compare yourself with someone else? Does it really matter in the grand scheme of things if you are similar or different from another person? Who really cares other than you at that moment in time? Probably no one. And what does it accomplish? Nothing. It is a waste of time to compare yourself to someone else. First, the comparison will probably be wrong because you don't really know all of the inner workings of that person and are probably just comparing outward appearances. Some people can put on a good act so you don't really know their true selves. Most people like their privacy and will put on a good face in public so that others don't know the problems that they're facing in their personal lives.

So, let's look at one of the examples I used above, "I wish I had his/her curly hair". My hair is curly and long and people tell me all the time that they'd love to have my hair. Well, it might look okay when they see it, but do you know how much *work* curly hair is? Not only is my hair curly but it also tends to be dry and tangles easily. That means that I can only brush it when it's wet (otherwise it will break) and even then it takes forever because I have to untangle it too. Hair product companies must love people with dry curly hair like me because you have to have moisturizing shampoo and conditioner—make it the sleek kind if you're trying to get rid of the frizzies (like me)—then add a leave-in conditioner, and mousse for curly hair to make it stay relatively in place and curl right. Then, let it dry by itself because if you put heat to it, it's going to puff up into the big hair of the 80's (which was great for me by the way!). Don't go outside if it's damp or raining because that's giving your hair permission to kink up, frizz and fuzz as if you'd just stuck your finger in a light socket. And don't forget to put it up in a bun when working with animals—pups and horses alike think it makes a great play-toy.

That example just goes to show that you don't really know what another person goes through to appear the way they do to others. Maybe someone who has a great body feels hungry all of the time just to look that way. Or maybe their life is spent working out when they'd rather be watching a movie. Or maybe that top executive that has it all together has a drug addiction or drinking problem that they hide from the world. See, you just don't know and you'll probably never know because people will try hard to hide things if they think it makes them look bad in someone else's eyes. Everyone has their own secrets.

Instead of comparing yourself to someone else, why not open your heart to your own inner self and take a good look at the wonderful things that make you who you are. If you don't compare yourself to someone else then you change your attitude and your perception. If you're a fan of comparisons, then compare two of your own qualities. Instead of saying, *I wish I had her hair*, get a perm and see how you like having curly hair. Then you can compare it to the straight hair you were born with and if you like it better, then keep getting perms, if not, let it grow out and go back to having straight hair. This is a way to transform yourself from the inside by making decisions based on who you are at your core being. Being thankful for yourself, even your flaws, will enable you to grow and transform and to move forward on your path.

Focusing on *yourself* is a positive transformative process. It's easy to get caught up in helping others, so much so that you might forget about what is important for you at times. You may put your goals aside in order to help others achieve their goals. There's nothing wrong with helping others, but sometimes, your inner self needs focus too. If you find that this happens to you, feel grateful for those people in your life that you're able to assist and then give thanks for your ability to help them. Turn the gratefulness inward and appreciate all of the hard work you do that makes you different from everyone else. Change your attitude to one of acceptance of yourself for who you are and you'll feel a transformation begin to take place.

As you're transforming, don't look to others for validation. You'll know what's right for you at a soul level without comparing yourself to anyone else. Be thankful for the unique, blessed, spiritual being you are and feel your confidence within as it shines to those around you. You'll discover that others will gravitate toward your light; they'll be drawn to your positivity and uniqueness. Give thanks for their individuality and your own as you focus on your transformation.

Turn Past Hurts into Gifts through Spiritual Gratitude

We've all been hurt or experienced emotional pain at some point in our lives. It's part of human nature because, by nature, we have a plethora of relationships with other human beings. When you're involved with people, from time to time, you're bound to have emotionally painful experiences. You may experience the pain of a breakup with a significant other or the pain of a loss due to death. You may be hurt by another person's actions or words even if you don't know them. There so many instances where we can experience emotional pain in life but it's what we do with that pain that matters most.

While there is no pill that you can take to ease emotional pain, or any magic formula that will erase hurtful experiences, spiritual gratitude can help in any painful situation. If you look at the situation from a place of thankfulness, then it can help open your eyes to varying viewpoints. You can see the situation from the other person's point of view, which may help you to come to terms with what has happened. Even if you can't see the situation clearly, if you can find a way to feel spiritual gratitude for some aspect of the situation, then it may help. Some situations are so horrendous that it is really, really difficult to move from the pain to a place of forgiveness or thankfulness. If you find yourself in a situation like this then you may benefit from professional medical help. Only you can decide the level of your pain based upon the intensity of what you've been through and if medical help is necessary.

If the situation is one that you can handle on your own, then you may be able to find a way to be thankful for being able to have had the experience in the first place. You don't need the other person's understanding or for them to be an active participant in your getting over the pain they caused you. They may never understand how you feel or comprehend your need to live by a certain standard or even realize that their actions caused you pain. You may go your separate ways for the rest of your life, or take a break from one another, or sometimes, through discussion, the issue can be resolved. Instead, let go of any negative energy their actions have caused you and allow yourself the freedom to forgive.

Let's look at an example. Let's say you've gained some weight and are having a problem losing it so you're sensitive about your weight. You're at a restaurant that has a buffet and you're the only one standing there getting food. A family is seated beside the buffet table and they have a small child. Then you overhear the child saying how fat the person is at the buffet table. The child could only be talking about you because you're the only one at the buffet. The parents shush the child saying that it's rude to say things like that and while the child is learning a lesson about being polite, your feelings have already been hurt. But let's say that you go home and decide to start on a diet the next day and within a few months, because of what that child said, you lose the extra weight. In this case, you can be thankful for the situation because it moved you to positive action.

Maybe you've been in a long term relationship that hasn't really moved forward to a level of permanent commitment. Then, you learn that the reason for this is because you're not the only person your partner has been involved with romantically. While this type of situation is always going to be painful because what you thought was truth ended up being lies, once you move past the pain and look at the situation with spiritual gratitude, then you might see things differently. Look at what you experienced during the relationship. Did you learn anything about yourself? Did you learn anything about relationships, trust, sharing, or commitment? Were there signs of cheating that you can see now but you didn't see while you were in the relationship? If you experienced joy at any time during the relationship, if you learned something about yourself or can now recognize warning signs of infidelity in future relationships, then you can be thankful for those things. By becoming aware of the aspects of the relationship for which you can be thankful, then you have grown spiritually within your own being and that's something that no one can take away from you.

Sometimes the most important lessons for us to learn in life are the most painful ones to go through. If life was too easy, if we didn't learn along the way, and if we weren't able to feel spiritual gratitude for the painful things in life, then we'd never grow personally or spiritually. When you look at painful events as a gift, and try to find the goodness within the pain, then you're being grateful for what that gift is giving you even though it might hurt. The same can be said for experiencing physical pain. If you get physically hurt, then you learn exactly how strong a person you are as you work though the physical pain to healing. You may discover that you're stronger than you knew you could be whether you're dealing with physical or emotional pain.

When you are able to appreciate the things that hurt you, sadden you and make you rethink what you believe, then you will gain inner strength. The stronger you become spiritually, emotionally and even physically then the easier it is to find ways to be grateful. We can't change how others treat us or prevent accidents from happening but we can change how we view the world and the people in it. The perspective you have now will be different and more positive if you add spiritual gratitude to your daily living. Instead of experiencing feelings of frustration or constant struggle you can look for the gifts you're given within those struggles and view them positively instead of negatively and with a profound sense of thanks. If you really want to accomplish this in your life, you will be able to do it through spiritual gratitude.

Become Worry and Stress Free

Transformation is often about letting go of preconceived notions of how you are supposed to behave in order to live up to the expectations of others. Instead you should focus on living your life in connection with your own inner truth. Transforming your way of thinking will often relieve stress and alleviate worry from your life.

I used to be a worrywart. It was bad. Really, really bad. I worried about everything, everyone and imagined every possible worst case scenario in just about every situation. And I was constantly tired from all of the worrying. Finally, one day, I decided that there really wasn't a reason for me to be constantly worried all of the time. I believe there is a reason for everything we do and experience in life and all of our experiences are helping us learn lessons that will move us forward on our spiritual path. If I believed these concepts—then why in the world was I still worrying all of the time?

It was because I wasn't living what I believed.

When I realized I had to release the worry to fully transform my actions to reflect my belief, it was like a light bulb moment for me. I understood that letting go of worry allowed me to feel content in all of the different situations in my life instead of fearing the worst case scenario. It was a welcome transformation. Changing my attitude from one of worry to one of acceptance wasn't easy. I had to open my heart to the positive thoughts and believe everything would be all right in the end because it was the way I'd planned it before coming to this earthly existence. And if it didn't turn out all right then there was a lesson in that too. I had to open my heart to spiritual gratitude and being thankful for having a life to live, mistakes to make and obstacles to overcome. I still worry about things at times and envision worst case scenarios—if I didn't I wouldn't be human. However, worry is no longer an obsession. I've realized that most of the things I was worrying about weren't ever going to happen anyway. I was wasting my time with worry when I could have been doing something constructive with it.

To be able to release worry and become stress free you have to be fully content within your own skin, which you've been working on throughout this book. You're probably more aware of your soul's purpose as you've been working on increasing gratitude in your daily practice and understand more deeply that everything in your life has a reason behind it. You've added more gratitude which has helped in your spiritual development. You are a blessed soul with many gifts from the Universe and from those you interact with on the earthly plane. Even if you experience suffering, you can be thankful for the experience because of the lesson within it. You might have to dig a little deeper for the lesson if you're in pain or having a bad experience, but if you adjust your attitude to one of gratitude and view the experience from the heart, you will find it.

Spiritual gratitude is important in changing your outlook from one of stressful worry to calm reflection. In addition to connecting to your spiritual self, there are other things that can help you to reduce the stress and worry in your life. Exercise, meditation, and keeping a journal (you can title one day's entry as *Get Out of My Head Worrywart!*) will help you get a handle on your stress levels and the amount of worrying that you do. Also, consider this question and write about it in your journal: What does worry accomplish? You know it causes stressful feelings of anxiety but what else does it accomplish? I'm not going to answer that question for you because I want you write freely, without limiting your feelings or what you say in any way. When you're finished go back and look at what you wrote. Do you notice more negative things than positive one? If you do, then you're probably worrying too much and need to change your outlook and make a loving transformation within yourself.

Experiencing stress is similar to beating your head against a wall. You're applying force to a nonmoving object and the result is pain within. With stress the force is your will and the pain is worry. Stress can cause physical problems just like beating your head against a wall will give you a headache, bruise or bleeding abrasion. Instead of being willful and trying to force life situations within a mold, let them flow in a positive way.

In order to begin a transformation of releasing worry and stress, begin with an open heart full of spiritual gratitude and look at your ideals and way of thinking. If you're worrying too much, just realize that most things are out of your control. Whatever happens, there is a reason for it. If you need to make changes on the physical plane that will aid in reducing your stress and worry than do it. For instance, if you are having a hard time sleeping, if you're not eating well or if you're not exercising—then change those things. Eat better, set a soothing atmosphere at bedtime and try to empty your mind to enjoy a better night's sleep. If you can stop your own inner struggle, it will help you focus on letting go of worry.

Become your own stalker by observing your reactions—are they negative or positive? Do they add to your stress and worry without your realizing it? It's easier to have positive reactions and less stress or worry if you're reacting with spiritual gratitude and thankfulness. Find time to experience silence (even if you need earplugs to do it) and then notice the thoughts that run through your head. Are they adding to your stress? Or can you find the answers you need within your soul essence? And finally, remember to stay true to yourself. If you're not, you'll become tired and irritable because of the disconnection within you. It will be hard to focus, easier to worry, and you'll feel more stress, which can be draining to your frequency. Become one with your natural essence, the peaceful part of *you* deep at the core level of *your* existence, within *your* subconscious spiritual being. When you release worry it's easier to become the thankful, loving and worry-free soul that you are at your core essence, it gives your life more meaning because the worry is no longer a block to living your own truth.

People Are Drawn to Your Spiritual Gratuitous Light

Every one of us is a being of light. Our souls are pure energy, our individual frequency, our personal vibration, is moving at a rate that is uniquely our own. The higher your frequency, the brighter your light shines into the world. Because we are trying to learn lessons that will further our spiritual growth, we're often attracted to others who vibrate at a higher frequency than we do. Being thankful and appreciative can raise your frequency and increase your light.

Have you ever met someone for the first time and immediately felt drawn to them? You may not even realize why you feel a connection to them (often this happens on a subconscious level unless you're consciously aware of frequency); you just know that you feel a connection to the other person's energy. You may find them easy to talk too or fun to be around. You may feel very comfortable in this person's presence but not able to put your finger on exactly why you feel this way. Your energy is drawn to their energy because their inner light radiates from them and attracts you. Have you ever been at an event and just felt the positive energy radiating off of a person you didn't know? If this happens in the future, stand back and watch what happens. Other people in the room will drift toward this person, engaging them in conversation because they too were attracted by their light.

When you meet someone who is at your same vibrational rate you probably won't feel this same kind of connection. Instead you may feel that the two of you have a lot in common, a familiarity with one another, as if you've known each other forever. Once you understand how connecting with another's soul energy works, then it's easy to determine when people have a higher, equal or lower frequency than your own.

Many people with higher frequencies often have psychic abilities, are mediums or have an innate understanding of the divine within us all. They are often teachers that help others understand their unique abilities. They may never come right out and say these things to you, but if you get to know them better, sooner or later you'll recognize their soul energy and know why you felt so drawn to them.

When you make spiritual gratitude a bigger part of your life and integrate it within your soul essence, you're living with a more open heart. You're thankful and share gratefulness with everyone you come in contact with during your day. Your light is shining because you're thankful and filled with joy.

Sometimes you may not know how to act when another person is drawn to your divine light in this way. That's why it's important to understand how your spiritual light affects others. If you're unaware, you might feel that the person is being annoying and won't leave you alone. You may dread being in their presence because you think they're being needy, when in fact, they are probably just enjoying your company and basking in the light of your soul. If you're aware, you'll understand there is something about you they need to connect with in order to understand or reconnect with some part of themselves. If you're aware, you can help them through this process by asking questions and being there for them.

I know I enjoy being around someone who is usually in a good mood, who is grateful, happy and comfortable within their being. They have a sense of peace and calm steadiness about them because they are connected to their soul essence, are living their truth and are filled with joy. It's more difficult to be around someone who isn't experiencing these things but when you're brought into contact with them it's usually because you will be able to help them in some way. Maybe you'll teach them about spiritual gratitude or frequency or help them see how brightly their own light shines. Notice how those of a higher frequency will usually treat you with kindness and are thankful for spending time with you. Take their lead and treat others in the same grateful manner.

Today one of my social media friends posted about a tribe of people who, when someone had done something bad, instead of seeking a punishment for the person, they gathered around him/her in the center of town and for two days, the other tribe members reminded the person of all the good within them. They believe that everyone is good and any misdeeds done are a cry for help. The tribe comes together to lift this person up emotionally, to help them remember their true nature that they have been temporarily disconnected from their own goodness. Whether or not this story is true it demonstrates a fundamental truth of our nature. We are all good inside, but sometimes we lose our way. What if we all helped one another remember the goodness within our spirit? What if we taught each other from the divine part of our souls and with spiritual gratitude and love? The world would be a much brighter place.

So what can you do to lift yourself up? Start with spiritual gratitude and acknowledging the blessings in your life. Open your heart to accept the thankfulness others give to you. Appreciate them for who they are and the importance they have in your life. Be thankful for yourself, for your light that shines brightly for all to see. Transform yourself by returning to your inner truth, your soul essence, the spiritual you that never dies for this truth will set you free from the confines of society and the limits of expectations. You are light, you are love, you are *you*.

—7—
Spiritual Gratitude During Difficult Times

Life is all about change. Spiritual gratitude can help you remain centered during transitions and other life changes so you can handle them with less stress and worry. We naturally experience difficulties on the physical plane of existence because that is the way we learn as spiritual beings. There are times when things go wrong, when we are sick or it feels like our world has been ripped apart. Spiritual gratitude can help you during all of these difficult times. Sometimes we just have to let everything shatter around us, be thankful for the experience and then pick up the pieces and move on. It's not always easy and can take effort on our part. Change happens to us every day; it's how we deal with it that counts.

Transitions, Changes and Spiritual Gratitude

Due to the world's current economic situations, there are many people in numerous countries who are experiencing difficulties. It's hard to be thankful when it seems like life just keeps throwing stones in your path to trip you up with every forward step you take. So how can you make it through trying times if you're struggling with feelings of fear, anger, frustration, anxiety and depression? You can make it through difficult times if you rely on spiritual gratitude. You might not be able to change the situations you're facing or affect the outcome but you can change your inner emotions associated with them and reverse your internal dilemmas.

When you use spiritual gratitude during difficult times, you're changing your circumstances by appreciating the problems you're facing. Think of the problems as experience you can learn from and be thankful for the lesson. You might not be able to see the lesson clearly because you're right in the middle of the situation, then again, you might or you might understand it in the future when you think about the experience. When you're spiritual grateful you're seeing situations from a perspective of mindfulness which can enable you to raise your awareness and consciousness. This helps you to see possibilities in the difficulties. If you maintain negative thoughts like fear, anger or frustration, then you're more likely to only see the negative in the situation you're in. If instead, you look inside your spiritual being, find the grace and calmness within you and then look at the situation from one of spiritual gratitude, it looks different doesn't it?

Let's look at an example. Right now, in the United States, the housing market is a mess. More and more people are losing their homes to foreclosure or their home is so upside down in value that, when the banks choose not to work with them, they're handing in their keys and walking away. You see it on the news every day. Some people have hundreds of thousands of dollars into their homes and that's a very difficult to walk away from. I've noticed (from what I've seen in the media) that people tend to take two different perspectives. Some are looking at the situation from a negative viewpoint and refusing to see anything positive in the situation, while others are looking at the situation in a positive manner and moving on with their lives. Either way, losing a home and the money you've invested to foreclosure can be an emotionally stressful time that's hard to move past. It is hard work to purchase a home and then put years into it and it's emotionally difficult to let that go when financial troubles occur. You might ask me how anyone could find something positive in this situation. Okay, first let's take a look at the family. Is everyone healthy? Could a move to a rental house or apartment take the stress of home ownership off of someone for a while and give them a chance to regroup? Could moving be considered a new beginning? A time to start fresh? Losing money or a home is never, ever easy but for those who try to find some positive in the situation through thankfulness of the other blessings in their lives, then the process may be more manageable. And you never know what great things are waiting for you when you move from one location to another!

Think about this when you're faced with a difficult situation; If you were at peace within yourself, if you could connect to your purpose in life, would you then feel more inspired to make a change even if that change is something that you might not want to do or that is being forced upon you due to hard financial times? Spiritual gratitude can do that for you. If you're unhappy in a situation or are feeling angry and resentful can you make an internal change as well as an external change? Sometimes letting go of the situation that is causing so much difficulty is the best option. If you're in a job that you hate, with co-workers that you don't really get along with, and you're taking those feelings home with you every night and making your family upset because you're in a bad mood—then why stay in that job? Maybe you'd be better off finding another job and then giving your notice to your current employer and leaving your old job behind. That change might be just what you need to become more joyful and happy.

Pressure from situations that we're unhappy with can really take a toll on us both mentally and physically. Anytime you find yourself in situations like this, first look at it with spiritual gratitude and make a list of the positives around you. Also make a list of things that you're unhappy with and possible outcomes based on different decisions you could make. Do any of those seem like they just *feel right* to you? If they do, then consider taking that path.

When you decide to look at difficult situations with spiritual gratitude, you're accessing your true spiritual nature. This connection can lift your spirits and make you more appreciative. Once you've done this and taken the most positive actions possible, and you've put those positive thoughts out to the Universe, then you just have to wait and see how things unfold. You might just get a positive, unexpected surprise where the situation completely turns around when you really didn't expect it to do so.

You can choose to be happy and thankful during difficult times or you can choose to wallow in despair and negativity. It's easy to get pulled into negative emotions but when you feel yourself spiraling down, pick yourself up with positive thoughts of thankfulness. Make a conscious choice to do something to move forward in the situation even if it's just changing the way you think about what you're experiencing. Feel your gratitude deep in your soul; be real in giving your thanks and you'll be amazed with the transformations that can take place. Those difficult situations might just become wonderful opportunities when you look at them in spiritual gratitude.

Spiritual Gratitude During Illness, Sadness, and Loss

Sometimes it's just downright hard to be thankful. Sure, we should try every day but quite honestly there are going to be days when you want to just stand in the shower and cry so no one can see you, when you don't want to have anyone else around so that you can feel your sadness, acknowledge your loss or just be sick or upset all by yourself. If that's how you're feeling, then that's *exactly* what you need to do.

Being thankful is a state of mind; it is part of your being just as psychic abilities are part of a person's being. I've often said that you can't get caught up in *being psychic* because then you lose touch with reality and your whole existence revolves around the psychic part of yourself instead of your true soul essence of which psychic abilities is merely a part. It's the same way with spiritual gratitude. If you get so caught up in *being thankful* instead of letting it flow from your soul outward, then you can lose sight of the reality around you. Sometimes you have to really feel your emotions to the depths of your soul, especially during times of illness, when you're sad or when you've lost someone or something that is important to you, in order to be able to give thanks during difficult times.

Sometimes, you don't need to think, you just need to be.

As I write this, we're smack in the middle of the holiday season. Thanksgiving has passed and Christmas is only a week away. As a nation, we're overcome by a horrible tragedy and our nation is in mourning. I've blocked my empathic abilities but still find that I'm sad, crying and extremely on edge and I can't seem to pull away from these feelings. It doesn't feel like the holidays to me this year. So today, I went to the barn and while brushing one of my horses I cried for all that has been lost by those around me in the past few months, I cried for the victims and families of senseless violence, I cried because I'm overworked and sleep deprived, and I cried until I couldn't cry anymore. Then, when I felt that calm stillness within me, when I found my balance on a spiritual level, I looked for what I could be thankful for in my life. At exactly that moment my mare decided to nuzzle my hand. I could be thankful for her and the foal she's carrying. I looked around my barn at all my animals. Yeah, I'm thankful for them. I'm thankful for my kids, my husband, my family, the weather, those little spiders who eat the flies, the breeze blowing through the barn, and I'm thankful for being alive so that I could have this experience.

In order to be thankful, you have to acknowledge loss, illness and sadness. By facing the struggles we can appreciate the challenges before us. Appreciating the difficult times gives deeper meaning to our thankfulness and our positive outlook on life. When you're looking at the situations you're struggling with, try not to dwell on them. Cry for them, acknowledge them but don't dwell on them for so long that you put yourself into a depression. Throughout life, struggles will pop up to challenge you—you'll get sick, you'll experience sadness and loss—it's part of living.

Getting past the grief of someone's death is difficult to do especially if it was a sudden, tragic death. As you go through this grief, you'll come to feel spiritual gratitude in your own time. You'll remember the good things about them and tend to forget the not so good, which we all have. In time, after you've gone through the anger, feelings of unfairness and that you've been cheated or deprived by the death of the person in your life, you'll then be able to see them as a gift. A blessing that was part of your life, regardless of the length of time they were with you. Once you can see past the natural feelings of grief to the other side of loss, then you'll come out stronger and with a new appreciation for all of the people who are gifts in your life.

When you consider how you can feel spiritual gratitude during times of illness, loss and sadness, consider this—it doesn't matter what kind of situation you're in or what kind of emotions you're feeling—you choose your reality. You can choose to live in a negative energy flow or you can choose to live in a positive one full of spiritual gratitude. We all have times where we're quickly plunged in the sea of negativity due to the circumstances life throws at us, but it is our choice to feel that cold water of negativity and quickly kick back up to the surface, jump out of the pool and dry ourselves off with the warmth of positivity, thankfulness, and spiritual gratitude. Or we can stay underwater and drown in a sea of despair. It's completely and utterly our individual choice.

Which will you choose?

It doesn't matter if you've made mistakes in your past. It doesn't matter if you've been submerged in negativity for months or years. What matters is the choice you make right here, right now, in this very moment. Your choice now can completely transform your life. You can lie down and wither away thinking that everything is going against you or you can choose to pull yourself together and kick some negativity butt! Be your own champion, be a winner in your own life. The potential is within you, all you have to do is choose it. During times of illness, sadness and loss, you can also become very aware, not only of your own inner spiritual self, but of the world around you. Even though you may not feel like it, sometimes these are the best times to change your perspective internally. Now I'm not talking about making rash decisions (during times of stress you shouldn't do that) but it's a good time to look within and examine yourself and your outlook on life.

When things are going well, we might forget about the blessings in our lives because we simply overlook them. We take them for granted. It's when things are going bad that we are very aware, analytical and observant (usually of the problems we're encountering). When they happen, the bad things in life can overshadow the good. Instead of thinking only of the bad things in a negative way, consider them a wake-up call to help you take stock of both the good and bad in your life and learn to appreciate all of it.

In times when positivity is abundant and flowing smoothly in our lives, we might overlook the little things—someone opening the door for you at the store, the smile of a child, a compliment, a gentle touch—simply because we're busy and going with the flow. In order to make spiritual gratitude work for you, the best time to be thankful is when things are going well. Try to be aware of the little things in life, the simple gestures from others that are a show of good will from one human being to another. These actions are powerful in their positive energy and when you're thankful for them, they can make your heart soar. When you're already living in spiritual gratitude, then, when bad things do happen or a crisis occurs, they will be easier to handle.

On the whole, as the human race, we all have love between us. We're kind, we're thoughtful and we care about each other at the soul level even if we don't always express it openly. We have a spiritual connection to one another through our soul essence. When we connect to each other and express kindness and that kindness is rewarded with spiritual gratitude, we're being who we truly are in spirit. To live a life filled with spiritual gratitude, start by being thankful when things are going well. Start with the small things, for instance, the kindness of strangers, your relationships with others, your health, or simply give thanks that life is going smoothly without problems. The fact that you are alive and can appreciate life through each of your five (or six) senses is something to be thankful for each day. If you're missing one of your senses, be thankful for those that remain. You can express this spiritual gratitude though your words and actions, which allows you to appreciate all of life through a renewed sense of joy and hope.

Sometimes tragedy is the catalyst to awakening and enlightenment. When something happens to us, we immediately and clearly see life in a new and different light. You may realize that the thing you're worrying the most over, doesn't really matter at all in the grand scheme of things. You may suddenly realize you no longer put importance on something that seemed like a big issue to you but you do care deeply about something or someone else and you see that clearly in the face of the calamity that faces you. Why wait for tragedy to happen to change your point of view?

It's very, very difficult to find a way to be thankful during these kinds of tough times, especially if there is a loss of life. How can you possibly find a way to be thankful when someone you loved deeply is gone? There are no words you can say to someone that will make them appreciate the fact that the person they've lost was in their lives when they're grieving the person they loved. Sometimes, less is more and just being a supportive friend who is there to listen is all you can do. Sometimes, well meant words can be misplaced. For example, if someone you know has lost a loved one, saying "at least they didn't suffer" or "at least they're no longer suffering", while meant well from your point of view, does little to ease their loss. Maybe just saying something like, "I'm here for you. I love you and will do anything to help you through this difficult time" would be appreciated more than the reminder of the loved ones suffering or not suffering. It's hard to be thankful when faced with death, but in time, once the grieving has run its course, regardless of how long that takes, eventually you'll be able to look with appreciation at all the joy the person who passed brought into your life. It takes time, but it does happen.

Death is a good reason to make sure that you're practicing spiritual gratitude in your daily life. Then, you'll have few, if any, regrets when someone dies. If you are grateful for the people in your life and express your spiritual gratitude to them on a regular basis, if you clear out any baggage that affects your relationships with others and express to them how much they mean in your life, then you'll know they knew you loved them, you won't have any regrets for things you didn't say but should have. Make it a point to say "I love you" every single day or multiple times in a day. Through spiritual gratitude, you've said and done daily what was right for you on a soul level and have cleared away negativity that may cause regrets.

As you try to mend relationships in your life, you may also run into instances where you are met with a brick wall. You reach out to another person to clear the air and they refuse to reach back. In those cases, you've done all that you could do to fix the situation and that has to be enough. As a spiritual entity you have to understand that we're all here to learn different lessons and to help one another with those lessons. Sometimes, the lesson is not yours but your involvement is helping someone else learn so they can grow spiritually. Take a few minutes today to look at your relationships to see where you can express thankfulness to another.

As you examine and are grateful for both the good and the bad things in your life, you will feel a sense of hope, joy and love for all that you've been given. Even in the face of tragedy you might find a new beginning. Life is what you make of it. If you choose to look at life with love, with thankfulness and appreciation then you will find yourself growing as a spiritual being and it will become easier to handle any obstacles that might cross your path.

Exercise: Find the Positive

For this exercise I'd like for you to think of a time when you went through a difficult situation. It may have happened a long time ago or be a recent event. Take out your journal and write one sentence that describes the event. It might be hard to get it down to one sentence especially if it was complicated. Once you have your sentence, change it from negative to positive. When you think of the event in the future, use this positive sentence instead of the negative way you'd previously thought about it. Here's a fictional example to show you what I mean.

Original sentence: I was unfairly laid off from my job without notice, am out of work and I bet it was because of something my co-worker who wanted my position said about me.

New positive sentence: Yesterday I was laid off from my job but today I'm going to find a better paying, enjoyable position working with happy people who work together as a team.

If you change your point of view you can usually find something good in a bad situation. You might have to dig deep to find it but there is something positive in everything that happens if you'll only look for it. Repeat this exercise for as many situations as you'd like to boost the positive energy around you.

Choosing to Move Forward

There are times when life doesn't throw sudden changes on you as indicated in the previous section, but instead, you decide that you need to make changes in your life because something you're doing or involved in is no longer working for you. While doing research for this book I came across an excellent model that was created by two well-known alcoholism researchers named J.O. Prochaska and Carlo DiClemente. In their book, *Changing for Good: A Revolutionary Six-Stage Program for Overcoming Bad Habits and Moving Your Life Positively Forward*, the authors outline a six stage model for change. After observing how people made changes in their lives, from overeating, smoking and problem drinking, they came up with this model and said that people who *self-change* are just as successful in their efforts to change as people who go to therapists or professionally run programs. I reviewed their model for changing problem behaviors and believe that you can also apply the basics of it to spiritual gratitude. I highly recommend reading their book because it's very in-depth and if you want to make lasting, lifelong changes their process would be very helpful. Let's take a look at the six stages in simplified form and determine how we can apply each of them to becoming more thankful.

1-Precontemplation: In this stage an individual may not even think they need to change. They may defend a bad habit, a deadbeat job, or any other negative situation they're in or behavior they have because they don't see it as a problem that needs changing or a situation they should move out of. For instance, if you're in a job that pays so little that you don't earn enough to pay your bills and the bank repossess your car, which leaves you without any way to get to work, then you should get a better job. But in this stage, the person in the situation will make excuses for and defend the job because they don't see it as a situation that needs changing. If others mention it they may think its exaggeration. If you apply this to being spiritually grateful, when someone says you should be more thankful your first response might be that you are thankful and who are they to say you're not? At this point, you may not even be aware or fully conscious that you're being ungrateful to the people around you.

2-Contemplation: People in the contemplation stage may think they *might* have a problem or be involved in a negative situation and this slight possibility gives a glimmer of hope for change. However, in this stage, people can't make a decision to change; they're just *thinking* about their situation, problem or behavior. They're not sure they really want to make a change or not or they may not have a firm grasp on what it is that they need to change in their lives. They may also consider the pros and cons of changing and look at any past attempts to change. At this point, they're thinking hard about the consequences of not changing even if they're not prepared to actually make the change yet. As applied to spiritual gratitude, you may become aware that you haven't been very thankful at a soul level, even though you say *thank you* often. You start to wonder how life would go if you were truly thankful for everything in your life instead of just saying thanks without really meaning it. You recognize and appreciate the need for change.

3-Determination/Preparation: In this stage the person actually makes the decision to make a change in their lives. They begin to prepare to make the change, and are ready and committed to take action. They're obtaining information, talking to others about how to make a change, networking and thinking of options for change. They are highly motivated and delve into research about how to make the desired change. Now you're reading books about how spiritual gratitude can change your life, you're talking to others about how they practice spiritual gratitude. You may even buy a journal, and look for spiritual gratitude exercises to implement.

4-Action: This is when the person puts their plan into action. They may make a public commitment, obtain supporters, or tell family and friends about their decision. They may try different techniques to make the change. They believe in themselves and are actively trying to change. People start to notice the change in them and may comment in positive ways. At this stage, you may have joined some online groups about practicing spiritual gratitude; you're following exercises from books, and trying to be mindfully aware to be thankful for everything in your life. You're journaling about the things you're grateful for and how being thankful connects to your soul essence.

5-Maintenance: This is when the person creates a new pattern of behavior over time with the threat of desire to go back to their old ways becoming less intense and less frequent. This is also the stage in which the person may relapse into old patterns of behavior. Because they know there is a possibility of relapse, they put systems in place to prevent it including help from family and friends if they notice the person is reverting back to their old ways. You might now notice when you've forgotten to be thankful, and immediately are; when you took something for granted and then gave thanks for it; when you let negativity in but then replaced it with positive spiritual gratitude. You may post notes around your workplace or home to remind you to be thankful throughout your day.

6-Termination: This is the stage when the old patterns of behavior are no longer a threat to the person. They know that they can cope without any fear of relapsing and the change is now part of their daily life. There is no worry about going backwards. This is also the time when, if a person has relapsed in stage five, they decide to start over with new techniques that may help them succeed the second time around or they revert back to the old pattern of behavior with no intentions of trying to change again. At this point, you've found that you've integrated thankfulness into your life. You may forget now and again, but you keep on giving thanks for all that is. If you've decided that being thankful isn't for you right now, you may relapse. But, that said, giving thanks is such a fundamental part of us as spiritual beings, relapses will probably be short lived.

Lasting change takes time, determination and persistence. When you decide to become more spiritual grateful, you're progressing along your spiritual path of positivity and oneness with your inner self. Soon, it will be second nature to you to be sincerely, truly grateful instead of just saying *thank you* without meaning it.

Reconnect with the Flow of Life

During times of transition and change it can be difficult to live in spiritual gratitude, especially if you're just starting to make this practice part of your daily routine. When you are able to move past trials and tribulations and move forward with appreciation for all you experience, you're essentially picking up the pieces and reconnecting with the positive flow of life. If you get stuck along the way, if you're trying your best but just can't get yourself out of a rut, then here are some little ways that you can act with purpose and spiritual gratitude to reconnect to your soul essence and the flow of life.

Mind your karma - In my experience, what goes around always comes back around. It may take a moment or years but what you give out will come back. Whether you call it *karma* or *just rewards* is up to you. To get through transitions and changes, always treat others with kindness and spiritual gratitude. You may not feel very grateful because of the things you're going through but if you treat people with respect and thankfulness, instead of treating them poorly because you're in a bad mood, then you will help yourself move forward faster and ensure that what comes back to you is positive.

Make a difference – Have you ever considered how much of a difference you can make if you help and are grateful for only one person at a time? When you're making a difference in someone else's life, it can help you see the things you're going through clearer. Giving of yourself by giving to another spiritual being, you're acting with pure positivity and even if you don't realize it that positivity will help you along your own path. Your time, your smile, and your assistance may mean the world to someone else. When my kids were young I always pushed a boat sized double stroller that weighed a ton and was filled with kids and kid supplies. For everyone who opened doors for me to push that bad boy through – thank you!! For me to get through doors I always had to back in, hold the door with my foot, pull the stroller through and then turn it around (which was not an easy task). The kindness of the random people who held those doors so I could walk right through meant a lot to me, even though it was just a show of kindness on their part. The little things you do can make a big difference.

Just smile – On every email that I write, I sign it "Smiles, Melissa". Some people think it's silly to send a smile in an email but I do it each and every time and have been doing it for many,

many years. Know why? Because I'm basically a happy person and I try to take a positive approach to life just like everyone else. When I smile, I simply feel better. When someone else smiles at me, it makes me feel better so I smile a lot too. It's a great way to spread happiness, even though an email. Sometimes we can get so caught up in our daily tasks that we forget to smile. The other day I was in a big store with one of my kids and we were rushing around getting last minute stuff for the holidays. I was exhausted and not feeling very well so I wasn't in a great mood. As we headed to the check out we passed by a family with a toddler sitting in the cart seat. That child was beaming from ear to ear and stared right at us as we passed by – well of course, I couldn't help but smile back and said hi to him. When I looked back, he was still watching us and smiling. That little boy in about fifteen seconds changed my mood from one of frustration to happiness because his own happiness was just overflowing from him. I smiled the rest of the day. Share your smiles and see if life doesn't flow smoother during times of change. ☺

Make amends – Have you ever done or said something and you were completely wrong in your words or actions? Sure you have! We've all done that at some point in our lives. We're going to make mistakes in life. When we do, it's how we handle those mistakes that matters. Mistakes can often throw us into times of transition. When you've done something wrong, then admit it, apologize for it, make amends and move forward in your life. When you don't do that, then you're stuck in the mistake. You may keep looking back at it with regret thinking of what you should have done or said to make things right. To prevent this, make amends. It will help you pick up the pieces of the mistake, fix them and move forward.

Don't lie – It's difficult to move forward in spiritual

gratitude and reconnect to the positive flow of life if you're living a lie. Honesty is the always the best policy in the overall scheme of things. You can be honest without hurting someone's feelings and without lies either. Have you ever wondered why it's called a web of lies? Because one lie leads to another and another just as a spider spins one piece of web at a time until they have an intricate maze of webbing. When you lie constantly you're placing lie upon lie and soon you aren't going to know the truth of your own being. Strip away all of the untruths in your life, get back to your true self and live in honesty. It takes more courage to be honest than to hide behind a lie.

Remembering these actions will make it easier for you to reconnect with the positive flow of life and to be grateful for yourself and those around you. Transitions will flow easier and change will feel positive and in forward motion.

—8—
Grace, Wisdom & Spiritual Gratitude

When you look at life with spiritual gratitude and grace, you will gain wisdom. They really work hand-in-hand and you can benefit from the combination. Knowledge is power, grace is a blessing, spiritual gratitude is appreciation for all that is and the resulting outcome is that you will grow and become a much wiser spiritual entity through your connection with them. There are hidden blessings all around you and you can change past pains into gifts by being thankful for them. Once you learn to look at life from the perspective of spiritual gratitude, the realm of the spiritual will speak to you as never before. Open your heart in thankfulness and accept the gifts you are given.

Hidden Blessings

Growing up, I remember being told, "Life never gives us a problem without also giving us a blessing". I actually don't remember who said it now but it was something I heard often along with, "If a door closes, a window will open." And it makes sense. If you look for the blessings and open windows when you have a problem or through difficult times, then those hidden positive treasures will help you act with grace and wisdom. You're looking at the positive, the good things associated with the problem instead of only looking at the negative. Spiritual gratitude, being thankful from your soul essence, can help you find these blessings and open windows. It can lift you from despair to hopefulness.

When I was about twenty-five years old, I'd gone out for Saint Patrick's Day. I'd been sick with bronchitis and was taking antibiotics so I wasn't drinking anything alcoholic. We only had a couple of little nightclubs in town and they all closed at two in the morning. But, since I'd been sick, I decided to go home early. I drove a 1969 notchback Mustang and boy did I love that car! My Dad and I had rebuilt it after it had been wrecked and it held great memories of us working together to replace the roof, priming and painting it. We also lived way out in the country, about twenty minutes from town, so the roads were dark with only some moonlight. As I traveled home, I kept my headlights on bright so I could see farther ahead. Suddenly, I saw a brown horse in front of me running in my lane. I slowed down and moved into the other lane and that's when my headlights reflected off of the black horse running along beside the brown one. I had no option but to slam the brakes, pull up the hand brake and donut the car to keep from hitting the black horse. It worked until the brown horse spooked and ran directly at me and slammed into the driver's side door which, since I'd done a donut the car was now facing that lane. By the time it was all said and done, the impact between horse and car knocked me out, and my leg was wedged between the hand brake and the console. When I regained consciousness, I looked for the horses and couldn't find them. Then I realized the danger I was still in because my lights were now out on the car and I was sitting in the middle of the road, in the middle of the night. So, I did what any other concussed person would have done; I turned the car around and drove the remaining four miles to our house without headlights, using the moon's light to guide me. When I arrived home, my parents called the police and I was taken to the doctor the next morning. My entire thigh, from my knee almost to my hip, was black from bruising; I had a concussion and ended up with post traumatic stress disorder.

I'm telling you about this event to illustrate how to find hidden blessings in problems in your life. If I look at this experience negatively, here's what I get: The car that I treasured was totaled. I had a concussion and PTSD (post traumatic stress disorder), the horse was hurt and I'd hurt the kind of animal I love most in this world, I had to go to therapy for the PTSD which I disliked, I couldn't walk without limping for weeks, I missed nearly two weeks of work, I flew off the handle a lot afterwards, people thought I was lying because it was my word against the horse owner and it was a very depressing time for me. I'll be honest, at first, I couldn't see any blessings in this event, but eventually, they showed themselves to me. I lost the car I loved but I ended up getting another newer vehicle, I didn't die in the wreck even though I was badly hurt and I healed, the horses didn't die and they healed, my parents took care of me instead of me having to take care of myself when I was hurt, I was aware because I hadn't had a drink and did some very defensive driving when presented with the second horse, I also had a new concept of how drinking and driving could be harmful years before all of the campaigns against it and was thankful that I hadn't been drinking that night, I learned to control my temper as a result of having PTSD, the concussion went away but left me with enhanced psychic abilities.

Whenever you are hurt, when you're spiritually grateful, you can see the positive in the situation. You may be forced to slow down, others may get to wait on you for a change if you're the primary caregiver, you may have visitors as you heal that you haven't seen in a while, or you may take the healing time to expand your mind through reading or writing. No one ever likes to be hurt or forced to slow down but if you can make good use of that time and see the blessings inside, then you're practicing spiritual gratitude. It doesn't matter what life throws at you, because it can throw a lot at once sometimes, as long as you remain thankful, positive and look for the hidden blessings in all that you encounter, and then you're succeeding in being spiritually grateful.

Spiritual Substance and Gratitude

Before we can discuss spiritual substance and gratitude we have to define what spiritual substance is. The dictionary defines substance as something that has mass, occupies space; is an essence or of an essential nature and has gist and heart. That goes right along with the spiritual part of you doesn't it? So spiritual substance is all that you are made of—from your physical body, spiritual body, soul, core spiritual essence and every single part of you that makes you a unique spiritual being. It is all of your feelings about yourself, your spiritual beliefs, your emotions and connection to your inner essence, higher self, core spirituality and most importantly your expressions of gratitude.

When you are filled with positive spiritual substance, then life feels like a feast. There is so much to learn, so much to share and even more to feel grateful for in your life. When your spiritual substance is lean, you feel more negative emotions, things don't go smoothly and life feels like a difficult road to travel. It would make sense then, in order to have a life that is as trouble free as possible, to live within the positivity that spiritual substance and gratitude offers. In denying the spiritual part of your being, the true core essence within your soul that is the real you, then you're denying yourself. When you are born, you only know your real spiritual self, and then as you grow you become acclimated with living on the earthly plane and the spiritual you can get lost within the human you. You can change this by expanding your knowledge of your own spirituality. You can reconnect with your spiritual substance and live in harmony with your own truth of being. In doing so, you're establishing positivity deep within you and life becomes easier because you are being true to yourself.

Think of spiritual substance and gratitude like an empty platter. When you're not connected to your spiritual, inner being, or if you're not even thinking about yourself as a spiritual being or learning more about yourself on this level then the platter remains empty. You may feel this emptiness as something lacking in your life or as a lack of gratitude. You might feel disconnected or as if things just aren't flowing well. You may have problems with work, relationships, or simply finding anything to be happy with in your life. But once you begin the path of discovering who you are as a spiritual being, then each discovery is something you place on the platter with thankfulness. As you become more aware of the underlying energies within you, the spiritual world around you, the gifts you've been given in life, any intuitive abilities you may have, your spiritual guides, your soul purpose, and viewing yourself not only as a human but as a spiritual being living in a physical body, then that platter gets full as you place each of these realizations upon it. What really matters in this lifetime is filling your platter full with spiritual substance and experiencing this lifetime to the fullest with your eyes wide open and in appreciation for all of the spiritual substance within you.

Spiritual substance is a living thing, it is our life force, our soul essence, all that we are and all that we can become. We experience it, feel it, embrace it and we share it with those around us (sometimes even if we don't know them), and we radiate it within our frequency by sharing of ourselves. When we acknowledge the truth of our being, and through the acceptance and appreciation of this truth, then we are growing in gratitude and spiritual substance. We are able to dually participate in both our human existence and our spiritual existence and to share both parts of a whole being with those we come into contact with while on the earthly plane.

If you feel as if you are lacking in spiritual substance, as if life is difficult to get through, then now is a good time to evaluate your platter of life. If it looks empty, then start making an effort to fill it up by purposefully and consciously taking charge of your own spiritual development. Only you can fill that platter and make a difference in your life. You have to take the first step to accept all of the spiritual gifts available to you. Start with research. Read as much as you can about as many different aspects of spiritual development that you can find. Some of it will feel right to you, as if it connects to your being as truth, and if it does, then it is *your* truth. You may feel this connection as contentment, happiness and joy. Sometimes it feels like a zing of energy flowing through you or you may experience the Chills of Universal Truth (these are deep seated chills that flow through you, indicating that what you experienced is one of your spiritual truths). When you are actively engaged in learning about your spirituality and yourself as a spiritual being, then you are experiencing growth and forward movement on your spiritual path—both of which fills your platter.

You are not in this alone. Many people have increased their

spiritual substance by sharing their knowledge and experiences with others. Right now, you may be learning and filling your platter but once the platter is overflowing you may start giving some of what you've accumulated to others. The gifts of knowledge, gratitude and sharing are the greatest items you can put on your spiritual substance platter.

As you expand your spiritual substance and gratitude you will become more aware and enlightened to the vastness of the spiritual realm, which is within you. The energy of love, peacefulness, contentment, happiness and centered fulfillment will surround you. When you live filled with spiritual substance and gratitude, you are truly being you. Your quality of life will change. What once seemed difficult now flows with ease. What once seemed impossible comes to fruition. Tears of sadness turn to tears of joy. Love abounds within you and happiness is yours.

Look At Life from a Universal Perspective

When you think about life in general what you do think about? Do you see it as the day in day out grind of responsibilities and the things you have to do to survive and pay your bills? Or do you see it as a pathway of living with purpose, meaning and direction? We all have to earn money to purchase food, pay for a place to live, to pay our bills and participate in fun activities. But if you only look at what you have to *do* in life, without considering the possibilities of all the unknowns, then you can find yourself in a rut. You may find it difficult to move forward and you may not give one thought to developing your own spirituality or sense of gratitude simply because you feel overwhelmed with the things you are obligated to do. Developing a Universal perspective to life doesn't mean you have to do more—there's only so much time in a day after all—but it does mean that you should try to think more and observe life from a Universal perspective of spirituality. When you do this you'll experience more feelings of spiritual gratitude because you're more aware of what you're thankful for.

When you look at life from a Universal perspective you're considering your own spirituality and the spirituality of others. You're looking past the daily grind and into Universal consciousness. You're considering that there is more to you than just the things that you do. Spirituality is your journey of self-discovery, of learning who you are at your core spiritual essence and appreciating yourself as a spiritual entity. Not only do you appreciate yourself but also those around you. When you view life from a Universal perspective you are keeping an open mind to possibilities instead of limiting your point of view to what you already know. You'll feel more connected to the oneness of being, which means you're part of something bigger than just yourself. You and everyone else on this planet, as spiritual beings, are also part of this Universal scheme. When you look at life in this manner, then it is easier to understand the differences in one another and to appreciate the uniqueness of every person you encounter. You see life as a continuous journey with direction and purpose, a quest to learn all you can as a spiritual entity.

Having a Universal perspective allows you to better understand yourself and the needs of those around you. It allows you to feel appreciation for what life gives you so that more opportunities can come your way. It's about unblocking any negative mindset you may have to allow free thinking of infinite possibilities. Thinking from a Universal perspective allows you to be an active participant in life not only with your physical self but with your whole being, physical and spiritual. It's like unlocking a door at the end of a dark tunnel and when that door is pulled wide open the tunnel is illuminated with light. All knowledge in the Universe is available to you; it surrounds you, fills you and can bring unlimited possibilities and opportunities and for that you can be grateful.

Spiritual gratitude is an important aspect of having a Universal perspective of life. When you think this way, you'll find that you no longer take things for granted but instead appreciate everything you experience. You understand your own faults, you no longer look at the negative but instead embrace the positive, and you have faith that everything will work out as it's supposed to be. You're no longer narrow-minded but are open minded to any and all possibilities.

Getting to the point in your life where you have a Universal perspective requires you to accept and to let go. Sometimes the things we hold onto the tightest are the things that limit our view and experiences. It allows you to give love and appreciation to that which hurts or disappoints you, thereby giving the hurt and disappointment permission to change to joy. It allows you to stay true to yourself, to your gifts and to doing what you feel must be done for you to be true to your soul essence. It is living with intention and focus on all that is possible. As spiritual beings we are recipients of Universal gifts and when we are thankful for these gifts, though having a Universal perspective of what we've been given, then the gifts keep coming to us.

When you change your perspective from a personal viewpoint where you're only noticing what you immediately experience to one of Universal perspective where there is no limit to what you can experience or encounter, you'll discover that your attitude toward almost everything changes. Instead of experiencing fear or dissatisfaction in life, you'll find these negatives will seem to effortlessly fall by the wayside to be replaced with spiritual gratitude and happiness. It's as if you're filled with grace and understanding and connectedness with thoughts, concepts and ideals that you may never have considered before. You'll notice the little things in life while considering a much bigger picture than you've ever thought of before.

Universal perspective opens your mind. It's like taking blinders off of a horse. When the horse is wearing the blinders it can only see what is directly in front of them but when those blinders are removed, they can see what is beside them and behind them, all at the same time. When you're no longer placing limits on yourself, and wearing your own blinders, and when you give your mind permission to consider all types of knowledge or to consider many different possibilities, then you can't help but grow spiritually and in spiritual gratitude. Life is short compared to the eternal universe so why not make the most of it while you're here? The possibilities are limitless if you're only open your mind to a Universal perspective.

Spiritual Gratitude Gives Second Chances

There are many times in life when we are given second chances. A *do-over* if you will. Think about your life for a minute. Have you had a lot of second chances? They can be as simple as being asked to repeat something that you didn't get quite right or something as big as being revived from death. Were there times when you gave another person a second chance even after they hurt you emotionally? Life is all about second chances.

Being spiritually grateful gives us the opportunity to have a second chance. To make rights out of wrongs by changing our perspective and seeing a situation from someone else's point of view. It gives us the ability to see things as they are and not as we want them to be and to be appreciative instead of taking things for granted. It enables you to see beyond yourself to see the other person as a spiritual being. We are each dependent on the goodness of others in the world. We are all human and we all deserve second chances sometimes. There is graciousness in each of us and allowing yourself to be gracious and see grace in others is showing your appreciation for yourself and the other person as spiritual entities.

Pain and suffering can often lead to second chances. In relationships, whether you experience the pain yourself and give another person a second chance or they give you a second chance, appreciate the value of reconnecting with that person. You may also be given a second chance at life after an accident. Understanding the fragility of our time here on the earthly plane is something we can be very thankful for. I always say life is short and that we must make the most of it while we are here.

There are other times when we are given second chances too. Maybe you really messed up on your job and expect to be fired, but your boss sees an honest mistake and lets you stay on, giving you the opportunity to redeem yourself and provide excellent work in the future. With the way technology is today, you have the opportunity to only put out your best work. You have a second chance to get it right before you put it out for the world to see. For instance when cameras weren't digital, you had less opportunity to get a good picture to present to the public. When we take pictures of our puppies it is very hard to get a picture that shows the puppy to its fullest potential. Puppies really squirm when you hold them, run away just as you take the picture or will sit and look at you so lovingly and then as soon as you snap the picture they jump toward you. It often takes us hundreds or digital pictures to get just one that is excellent. These are second chances to get the best picture.

One area where it is difficult to get a second chance is when you're meeting someone new. I've often heard that you never get a second chance to make a good first impression. While technically that is true—you can't redo any *firsts*—there have been times when the second impression that I had of someone was much better than the first. We never know what's going on with someone the first time we meet them. Maybe they've been sick, had an argument with someone or they just got pulled over by the police for speeding right before you met them. Any situation in life that could cause a person to be upset or not feel well can affect how you perceive them the first time you meet. That's why it's important to always give someone a second chance before you finalize your impression of them. They may be very grateful for your kindheartedness in giving them an additional opportunity to make a good impression with you.

Second chances fill you with sincere spiritual gratitude. After the initial event you may realize you were wrong. Admitting when you're wrong isn't always an easy thing to do especially when it is something that has a tremendous effect on your life or on someone else. But if you can be grateful when you've been given the gift of the opportunity to correct a mistake, then admitting errors come more easily.

If you are mindfully aware that each person on this planet is a spiritual being, regardless of sex, race, skin color or beliefs, if you can see past all of the outwardly appearances or actions you may disagree with to the spiritual entity at the core of each human being, then you can truly appreciate each person for who they are at a soul level. I believe we all deserve more than one chance to interact with one another. You may not resonate with a person the first or second time you meet them but maybe on the third time you realize this person is in your circle of souls and a deep friendship forms. Had you not been given those additional chances of interacting, you may not have realized the connection you have with them.

Second chances are opportunities we should be grateful to receive, not something we feel entitled too. They are gifts that humans give one another in order to interact on a more spiritual level. They are also blessings we are given from God and the Universe to do more with our lives than we may have been doing previously. Whenever you are given a second chance, be thankful and express your appreciation to the person who gave it to you. If you have the ability to give someone else a second chance, then do it. Let the person know you appreciate them and feel they are worth a second chance. Second chances allow you to connect on a deeper level with the people in your life. Sometimes second chances are in the form of forgiveness. You may not be able to let the person be a regular part of your life but you can forgive their actions or words.

Heal Your Soul

There is a lot of negative and positive energy in the world that can affect us on a daily basis, especially when it comes to our own personal frequency. Sometimes we don't even realize what's going on. Using spiritual gratitude you can align your soul back to where you should be on your spiritual path by changing negatives into positives to bring about transformative healing.

If you find you're lacking motivation, feel you have no direction in your life or if you're frequently feeling sad or helpless then there's no better time than right now to take control and through spiritual gratitude change the way your life is going. The choice is yours. It's entirely up to you. Either you can continue along a negative path or you can turn in a new direction and follow a path of positivity.

Take a minute to think about this: isn't it better to live in the light of positivity then the darkness of negativity? Sometimes we end up surrounded by negative energy and don't have a clue as to how we got there. Negativity is like a thief in the night—it can sneak up on you when you're not looking.

There are times when we're not being mindful or in sync with our own feelings of spiritual gratitude. We're just moving along as if in a haze, without really connecting to our inner light. When this happens, we're often unhappy and have feelings of low self-esteem. Negativity can do that to you.

So how do you get out of it? You begin by replacing any negative thoughts that pop into your mind with positive ones. For every negative thing you think, say out loud the positive opposite of the negative thought and add gratitude. If you think your hair looks ugly then say, "my hair is beautiful, it just needs a new style." Appreciate the negative thought for making you notice this particular thing about yourself and then go get a haircut. If you think that you're overweight then say to yourself that you are a slim person on the inside and start working out and eating healthy to lose weight. Be thankful for each of the negatives your mind throws at you because you can react to each and every one of them in positive appreciation.

The other key element here is appreciative action. When your mind throws negatives your way, then be prepared to counter with a loving, grateful, positive thought and to take action to bring that positive to fruition. You have to make a conscious effort to replace the negative thoughts with positive ones, but you can do it if you set your mind to it. Not only will you feel more balanced spiritually but you can experience the positivity of spiritual gratitude at work in your life.

Many times the negatives you experience may not apply to you but for some reason, probably even unknown to you; you absorb the energy associated with the negative situation. This usually happens when there is an external situation going on. For instance, let's say you're at work and your boss is going on a rampage. He got in trouble because your division isn't producing as expected by the corporate office. Your work has been exemplary but not everyone in the office works to the best of their ability. While you know the boss is mad because he's in trouble, if you take his words as a negative personal attack against your productivity, even though it's high level work, then you're letting negativity that doesn't apply to you affect you internally. While you can show spiritual gratitude toward your boss and to the corporate office for pointing out the low production so your division can improve, you don't have to internalize his harsh words and feel bad about yourself. In this situation, you could offer to assist other workers to give them tips for increasing their own productivity to show your spiritual gratitude.

It is important to use spiritual gratitude to turn negative situations around, to release negative thought patterns and to fight stress, which is negative energy pushing down on you. When you find ways to be thankful for any negativity in your life then you're helping to heal yourself from within. Too much negativity in the mind can be the cause of worry and stress. Too much stress isn't healthy and can lead to physical health problems. Our minds can sometimes feel as if they're going ninety miles an hour and are near impossible to stop. If this happens to you, then find a quiet spot somewhere (outside is always good if the weather is nice because communing with nature seems to make it easier to release negativity) and work on quieting your mind. Slow your mind down and then address each thought by lovingly embracing it with spiritual gratitude and then release it. As you do this with each issue, your mind will quiet down. Breathe deeply and allow the cleansing energy of the air to flow through you while you express your thankfulness for its life giving properties. (As a side note: If you're having trouble sleeping because your mind refuses to slow down, use this same exercise in bed to help you fall asleep.)

At times you'll encounter people who are just miserable. They want to pull you into their misery so they'll have company. If you encounter people like this then you really have to determine whether or not being connected with this person is healthy for you. In some cases you can have the opposite effect and you can help them turn their lives from negative to positive, but at other times, no matter how hard you try to teach them about the positive effects of being spiritually grateful and adding spiritual gratitude as a part of their daily routine, they don't want any part of it. This is often because it can be uncomfortable to transform negative feelings to positive ones. Sometimes it hurts to face truths about yourself but doing so brings positive internal changes. If someone isn't ready to walk that path with you, then you may have to leave them behind. They might catch up sooner than you think but in the meantime, just keep working within yourself.

Feeling spiritual gratitude for difficult situations will allow you to make a total transformation within your spiritual core. This is especially true if you allow the negativity of others to have a negative effect on your soul. Reverse the energies and feel the power of positive thankfulness within your being as you replace negatives with positives and heal what ails your soul.

The Miracle that You Are

At the core of your essence is innermost being, your soul, which is who you really are in spirit. Your inner light radiates from your soul and shines into the world for all to see. Each spiritual being is a miracle. I believe we are each part of God and we are always in a constant state of transformation striving to eventually reunite with our Creator. Spiritual gratitude is part of our core essence because through thankfulness and appreciation we are able to move forward on our spiritual path to once again become part of all that is, a greater consciousness of being.

Each of us is born with a unique personality that reflects our spirituality. If you are connected to your spiritual self, then the miracle of you will always shine through your personality. We are each different in our own unique ways. We all have different physical appearances, mannerisms, a unique laugh and manner of speaking and we all love in our own individual way. We each express our spiritual gratitude differently too. Some of us are very touchy-feely and enjoy communicating our spiritual gratitude through hugs, pats on the back or squeezing someone's hand. Some of us are more verbal and tend to express our thanks through the written word or though speech. Most of us are a combination of both. It doesn't matter how you express your gratitude to others as long as you're doing it.

It can be easy to forget our uniqueness but sometimes you should stop and think about how exceptional you are. If negativity has affected you and you feel like you're not good enough, or pretty enough or smart enough, just stop for a second. Who are you comparing yourself too? Since you are a miracle, a joy and an expression of your distinctive spiritual being you don't have to compare yourself to anyone else. You have purpose here, you are part of a bigger plan and you are definitely unique. Be grateful for your incomparable spiritual essence and the bright light of love and happiness residing inside you. When you can see yourself as the miracle that you are, then you can share your uniqueness with others. If you're not seeing yourself in this way, then you may tend to hide on the sidelines of life instead of living it to the fullest extent possible.

When your spirit came into being in the spiritual world, you were made exactly as you were supposed to be. When you were born into the physical world, you are still exactly as you are in the spiritual realm, a unique individual entity, except now you're living in a physical body. With or without the restrictions of the physical you will always be you. Appreciate who you are and don't let what someone else may or may not think about you affect you in any way. If other people can't see the miracle that you are, then they're not seeing the miracle within themselves. Once you see yourself as a miracle and appreciate your uniqueness, then you can't help but to think of everyone else you meet in the same way.

Exercise: The Uniqueness in You

If it's difficult for you to see yourself as a miracle then try this exercise. This exercise is twofold. First I want you to stand in front of a mirror and look into your eyes—do you see your uniqueness; can you see your own soul essence and be thankful for being who you are? Remember what you're thinking when you look at yourself.

I've told you that I love lists so we're going to make another one. This time I want you to write down every single thing you can think of that makes you unique—whether you feel it's an attribute or a flaw. Write down everything that you thought of while you were looking at yourself in the mirror. If you want, look at yourself again with a pen and paper beside you and write your list as you're examining yourself. You may share characteristics with other people like hair color or eye color, but what makes your eyes or hair distinctively yours? Are you a brunette who goes into the sun and your hair has red highlights? Or do you have green eyes with flecks of gold in them? You can find differences in shared characteristics that are unique to you. For instance, my eyes change colors. Weird, I know, but that's just me. I actually think it's pretty cool. One minute my eyes will be hazel, another time they're blue and still other times they're a brilliant green. I can even make them change on demand by closing my eyes and pressing on my eyelids. (My kids love that trick!) Are you a great listener? Are you an exquisite cook? Can you write a song, rope a cow from horseback, put your feet behind your head? Are you honest, open-minded, sharing, committed, loud, quiet or all of the above? Each of these things makes you unique and you can probably come up with hundreds or maybe even thousands more. While you're making your list think of every miraculous thing about yourself and write it down. Once you've finished (and take several days to make this list because you'll keep thinking of more you can add) then go over it and give thanks for each item individually. Take the time to truly appreciate yourself.

 None of us are perfect and it's that imperfection that makes each of us unique spiritual entities. We're all here doing the same thing, becoming better, learning more and connecting with the divine within us. If you remember this, you'll find that you're less likely to judge others or to have negative views about them. We are all the same—unique, miraculous and spiritual. Believe in yourself as a miracle, love yourself and if others see the miracle within you that's fantastic, but if they don't, you know what is within you. To really understand how unique and miraculous you are, you have to accept yourself with all of your flaws and gifts. When you love the unique spirit within you, then it's easier to let your positive light shine to others. Creating this list while examining your essence will help you see, accept and love every part of yourself.

―― 9 ――

Practice Joyful Living in Spirit Every Day

Do you practice joyful living through spiritual gratitude every day? When you are spiritually grateful you are giving thanks for something that has brought you joy. You are open to the spirit of others and feel a need to give back in some way. You may find you enjoy being of service or you enjoy experiencing spiritual gratitude in other ways. Joyful living in Spirit is following your divine path. Are you ready? Then let's find out how much joy spiritual gratitude can add to our day!

Building Gratefulness in You and Thankfulness in Others

The opportunity to give is an opportunity to nurture spiritual gratitude within yourself and allow it to spread to others in a pleasant way. When you give of yourself and of your time, you feel joyfully rewarded and gratified at your spiritual center. Sharing your energy with another person or a group of people while participating in a project can be fun and entertaining. There are many times when gratitude is the catalyst for an opportunity to give.

Donate Money: One of the easiest ways to give, and one that doesn't take up a lot of time, is to donate money to your favorite charity or other cause. Some people have an extremely busy schedule, which makes it difficult to donate their time, but it only takes a minute to sign onto a charity website, click a button and make a monetary donation. You can also sign up do donate a specific amount each month so that it's done automatically through your bank. When you donate money you're helping businesses to provide necessary services for those in need to have the things they require to live (food, shelter, clothing etc), to support medical research, to support our veterans, and well, the list is endless. You can also do something even more personal when you donate money. You could choose the amount of money you want to give, go out into a public place, pick a person who you feel drawn to and just hand them the money. They'll probably be flabbergasted and refuse to take it at first, so just explain something along these lines, "I've decided to do my part to help others in the world by picking one person at random each day and giving them some money as a gift. Today, you are the person I've chosen. Thank you for being you and have a blessed day." There's not much they can say to that except thank you.

Being generous with tips when you're dining out at a restaurant is another opportunity for you to give. When I worked as a waitress I once received a one hundred dollar tip. The people had been at the table for hours and I had a great time serving their food and making their dining experience a pleasant one, but I never expected that kind of tip. That's not much by today's standards but when I was eighteen a twenty dollar tip was considered a lot but a hundred dollar tip? I'd never heard of anyone getting that much before. I was very grateful for that tip because it was so unexpected and because it let me know how much the people had appreciated my service. Because of that experience, today when dining out I always leave a much more generous tip than the minimum expected especially if we've gotten exceptional service.

If you have free time you can donate to a cause or charity, then you could either participate in a planned event or you may choose to start your own. I know in our local neighborhood there are several people who hold bike drives during the holidays. People donate their old bikes, which are then fixed up and painted and given to needy families with children in the community. Some people will load up all of the bikes and take them to neighboring towns and cities where the population is bigger and there are more people in need. This is a great event that helps a lot of people. It also gives you many opportunities to give. You could give of your time and help with the organization, restoration or deliver of the bikes, you could donate a bike, you could donate paint, tires, accessories or an air pump, you could help find families in need and provide a list of their names and addresses to the organization running the bike drive. See how many opportunities to give are within just this one event?

You could also do events on your own. Maybe you'd like to host a bake sale and donate all of the money to your favorite charity, or you could buy a bunch of dog and cat food and donate it to the local humane society or pet food bank, or you might like to do your own bicycle drive. There are many ways you can give to charities and other causes if you'll only look around you to find those in need. Find an event near you or create your own and involve yourself in helping others. You will be filled with gratitude because you helped feed an animal for the day, because you had a bike to donate or you could be thankful that you're a good cook who could donate to the bake sale. In appreciating your ability to help, you'll be filled with joy which will connect to your spiritual consciousness. You will be pleased with what you've been able to do for another person and they in turn will more than likely be very grateful for your help and will pass those good feelings to someone else.

Volunteering: Another opportunity to give is when you offer your time through volunteering. It could be any kind of volunteering from helping your neighbor clear leaves out of his yard to helping a kid with his homework or helping during disasters. Giving of your time is giving of your energy and spreading your positive sense of gratitude to those around you. Not only is giving of your time healthy for you and makes you feel spiritually connected to other people in the world but it gives you a sense of belonging to something bigger than just your life. It allows you to see the needs of others and to do something to bring a little joy into their lives.

Finding opportunities to give is easy if you'll look around. All you have to do is pick one and go for it. You'll be appreciative to help out and the person, cause, or community you've assisted will be thankful too. If you get stuck and don't know where you could find opportunities to give, then think about the kind of things you like to do. If you love horses, find a barn that will let you hang out and muck stalls or groom the horses. Or if you love spending time with the elderly (they are very wise and can teach you a lot) then find a nursing home to visit. The hospital and library are also great places to volunteer. Take your interests and turn them into positive opportunities to give in appreciation to those around you while sharing a reason to be spiritual grateful to others.

Participate in The Arts to Stimulate Spiritual Gratitude

Before we get into how spiritual gratitude and the arts go hand-in-hand, let me just say that if the arts aren't your thing but history or science is, then you can apply what I'm talking about in this section to any particular area of interest that appeals to you.

Let's define what The Arts are. When you think of art you probably think of paintings and you'd be right. But *The Arts* includes much more than just paintings. There are Applied Arts, Decorative Arts, Fine Arts, Liberal Arts, Performing Arts, and Visual Arts. There is some disagreement over what each of these terms covers because there is so much overlap within The Arts. At their core they cover dance, ballet, music, drama, film, theater, digital design, creative writing, poetry, interior decorating, ceramics, painting, sculptures, and so on. When you refer to The Arts, you are referring to any outlet that allows you, as a spiritual being, to express your creativity and imagination into the design or creation of an end product that others can enjoy and appreciate.

Participating in The Arts not only allows you to learn something about yourself on a spiritual level or your unique talents, but it also allows you to be grateful for those you teach you how to bring those talents to the forefront, those who enjoy the finished product and the divine path you walk between the beginning and end of a project. In the arts there are often nerves involved and I believe having our nerves on edge often leads to a better quality performance. Sure you relax once you get on the stage and see all of those people intently watching your performance but the nerves you feel before you enter stage right makes you feel spiritual gratitude that the time is at hand to deliver your best performance. You can probably tell from this paragraph that I was a theatre major. I loved performing and the work behind the scenes designing costumes and stages. It really gave me a great appreciation for what goes into movies, major theatrical productions, and musicals. When you can, though your performance or your painting or other type of artistic endeavor, connect to the soul of another person and make them *feel*, then there is extreme spiritual gratitude in that.

The arts can affect you in many ways. They teach you to think about things differently, affect your emotions and your intellect. They allow you to connect with your senses and to dig deeply into your well of spiritual emotions to find a divine connection to the experience. You can show your spiritual gratitude for the arts by taking a trip to a museum, attending the screening of a new film, support an indie project, and watching a theatrical production. You can also take part in community painting classes to release your inner artist. The arts stimulate the creative essence within your soul.

You can participate in the arts in two ways—as an observer or as the artist. When you are the artist you are using your innate talents and letting your spiritual essence shine. You will experience spiritual gratitude because you have the ability to give joy through your art. Spiritually, we've always been entities of expression; we've always found a way to bring the colors, the sounds and the energy from the spiritual realm into the physical. Today we call it The Arts but in earlier times it was through cave drawings, dance and song. Creative expression of our inner selves has always been an important part of being the spiritual entities we are because it enables us not only to reconnect to the part of our immortality but to find a clear way to express our spiritual gratitude for ourselves. It doesn't matter if you're a participant or observer; the fact is that you're engaged in the expression of your spiritual essence on some level.

Sometimes the act of creating your artistic creation is part of your divine path. For instance, let's look how spiritual gratitude can affect an artist who paints or takes photographs. The painter must have the creativity to put pen/pencil to paper or paint to easel in a way that expresses what the artist sees with their eyes. The photographer must know the exact moment to snap the shutter in order to capture the essence of their subject. Both have the opportunity to take their craft into nature, to listen to the sounds around them as they paint or take pictures. I believe sounds are part of the creative process. When you're in tune with the natural world around you, then the frequency of the world blends with your own personal frequency and creates a higher level vibration during the time you're creating your painting or photographs. As the artist, you can't help but feel spiritual gratitude for the objects you are painting or taking pictures of, because without them, you wouldn't be participating in the artistic endeavor. When the finished product is shown to others, they too will feel the spiritual connection between the end product and the frequency within themselves which creates appreciation.

    If it's been a while since you've actively participated in the arts, then find an event near you and plan to attend. I know one of my favorite ways to participate is during our local renaissance faire that is held every year. It is a lot of fun to watch the plays during the festival and the short impromptu skits you'll encounter while walking around. What's even more entertaining is when they pull you from the crowd to become part of their production. This kind of enjoyment, happiness and spontaneity can't help but fill you with spiritual gratitude for those actors and their ability to engage their audience. Whatever way you choose to surround yourself with the arts, remember to show your appreciation and spiritual gratitude for the artist's ability and the fact that they took the time to be creative so you could have an enjoyable experience. You might just be inspired by them to explore your own creativity in the arts to go from observer to participant.

Be of Service to Others

When you are of service to others it means you are giving freely of your time, energy and spirit without expecting anything in return. Being of service to others can help you bring spiritual gratitude to the forefront of your life. There are many people who need assistance, and some may have a difficult time asking for it or accepting it even when it's freely given. Helping others, like spiritual gratitude, is a core part of our divine being. We can't go through life without assistance so being of service to others is an essential part of our growth. Spiritual gratitude raises the level of awareness for you and the person you're helping.

As you offer your assistance, be genuine in your desire to help. If you're just going through the motions because you think it's something you should do but you don't really feel a deep desire to be where you are and doing what you're doing, then you're just giving it face value instead of really feeling it within your spirit. Offer your services consistently each day. You may already be of service to those close to you on a daily basis but can you expand your sharing of yourself outside your own circle of souls? Reaching out past your comfort zone not only gives you the opportunity to experience greater amounts of spiritual gratitude but it also pushes you just a little further down your own spiritual path by allowing you to meet new people and have new experiences because you were courageous enough to leave your comfort zone.

Serving others can happen in many different ways. You may be emotionally supportive, give good advice, teach or be a sounding board when someone needs to vent. Serving others doesn't always have to do with giving but can be a way to connect spiritually with someone. You may be to help someone learn to go with the flow of life instead of constantly fighting against their natural current. You may help someone overcome vanity or shallowness by offering a broader, deeper understanding of the spirituality within all of us.

You see, it is what we do during our time on the earthly plane that matters. Living apart from your spiritual self doesn't allow you to develop the kind of loving, gratuitous, and self-less emotions that are important to your growth. When you're being of service to others, you will naturally choose options that align with your own spiritual values. For instance, if you're living in spirituality you wouldn't help someone rob a store would you? Obviously not. Even if you're not living in spirituality but are a moral person, you wouldn't choose to become a criminal because that would go against what you believe to be right according to your own values and ethics. Instead you would choose offer your service in the light of unconditional love. While our thoughts, beliefs, thankfulness and love are all important in this lifetime, our actions, acts of kindness and service for others make the most impact on the lives of the people we come into contact with. You've probably heard the saying that actions speak louder than words and it is so true. You can *say* anything, make any promise, but if you don't live up to those words and keep your promises through your actions, then you might as well keep your mouth shut. Sometimes all that is needed are words but the majority of the time your action reinforces the words you say.

Being of service to others is all about the intention behind the service. The best intention is when you want to help someone and don't expect to receive anything in return. But if you say you want to be of service and don't want anything in return but are secretly hoping and wishing that other people notice how much you're being of service, and then you're disappointed when they don't mention anything about how great you are for doing what you're doing…well guess what? You're doing it for the wrong reasons because you're only being of service to make yourself look good in someone else's eyes. That's not what being of service is about.

You can also make the mistake of taking the idea of being of service too far. It is one thing to truly want to help someone and another thing to do so much that you're being taken advantage of by the person you're trying to help or you're not giving them the opportunity to do something that will serve as an opportunity to learn. You don't have to suffer for a cause in order to give in the service of spiritual gratitude. If you feel your being of service to others has made a turn in the wrong direction, then it may be time to pull back from that specific service and turn your attention to another way where you can help someone and really make a difference. It's a hard call to make sometimes so it's important to pay attention to the affect your actions are having at the place where you're offering service. When you overdo it, when you provide the service for so long that it becomes an expectation on the part of the other person, then it's time to end it. Expectations can hold you back because it's easy to let someone else consistently do things for you instead of doing for yourself. But that's not the most beneficial path to take because it can make you lazy and disconnected from your soul purpose.

When you think of being of service to another person, don't over think it. Physically being present at an event that is important to someone else even if it's inconvenient for you is being of service. They will probably be very grateful that you showed up to support them even if you're not expecting their spiritual gratitude in return. Listening or giving a hug when words can't express the wealth of emotion during difficult times is also being of service. Think of times when someone was being of service to you. How did you feel? Were you grateful that someone came to your aid just when you needed it and when you didn't expect it? I believe these are the most precious unexpected moments in our lives that we should truly savor.

Give Back through Random Acts of Kindness

Random acts of kindness is when you attempt to make the world a better place by being selfless and doing something to help another person just because you want to do it. When you are kind to another person you are mindful of how your actions are affecting someone else and you're acting with purpose to bring joy into that person's life. Random acts of kindness can be given to anyone, whether you know them or not, and it often happens with people you've never met before. Random acts of kindness often affect the person you share your kindness with and they in turn are kind to another person. It's a wonderful way to show your spiritual gratitude for someone as a spiritual being. You're acknowledging them as worthy of kindness.

Never underestimate how powerful random acts of kindness can be. Suppose the person you're kind too is having a bad day but your kind gesture elevates their spirit and allows them to feel spiritual gratitude. It's really a winning situation for everyone involved. You feel good for sharing and they feel good for being on the receiving end of your kindness. When you're kind to someone else, you're recognizing that your attitude and actions are positively affecting another person. You're holding yourself accountable to living in spiritual gratitude as a spiritual being and even if your kindness isn't reciprocated, you're growing as a spiritual being by sharing of yourself. That's really a great way to go through life isn't it? Kindness generates spiritual gratitude and positivity for everyone involved.

Let me give you an example of something that recently happened to me. I was in line at the grocery store (yes, I'm in line a lot!) and there were two people in front of me. The person at the checkout was elderly and having a problem getting the debit machine to take her card. It was taking a long time and the person in front of me was getting very frustrated and irritated. Because of the actions of the second person, the clerk kept apologizing to everyone waiting. The clerk helped the person with the debit card issue and then took the next person in line who complained the entire time. When it was my turn the clerk still apologized but I told her that I wasn't in a hurry and it was okay. I engaged her and the person behind me in conversation and by the time I was checked out, we were all talking about something else and the incident was forgotten. But when I went out the door, the first person was standing there with her cart trying to get the card back into her purse and was obviously upset. I didn't know why but thought it might be because the second person wasn't very nice in their comments. She looked up at me and I said to her, "You know, my card always gives me problems too. I'm surprised that you got it to work so fast! It normally takes me much longer." She looked at me and said, "Thank you, dear. That is so nice of you to say." So I gave her arm a little squeeze and said, "Don't you worry about what that other person said. Maybe they don't have ornery debit cards like we do." We talked for a few more minutes and then wished each other a wonderful day. As I walked away I heard her give a big sigh and she started to hum and push her cart. I have to tell you, that whole exchange made the rest of my day very positive, simply because kindness diffused the negativity of one person, which had affected several people, and replaced it with positivity.

It's easy for negativity to spread quickly especially in group settings. In times like these offering random acts of kindness can turn things around just as quickly. The key aspect of random acts of kindness is that you do them without expecting anything in return. You'll often be surprised by the spiritual gratitude and positive feeling that come right back to you just as quickly as the kindness you gave away.

To give back through random acts of kindness try to make it a habit to do it daily. There are many ways that you can be kind to others. One of my favorite random acts of kindness happened recently happened a lot. I heard about it from several people and thought it was a wonderful way to spread happiness. It's when people pay for something for someone else when the receiver has no idea it is going to happen. People are going through the drive through at fast food restaurants only to discover the person in front of them has already paid for their food. Or, they've gone to get their items out of layaway only to find out it's already been paid off. Or when it's time to pay at a restaurant, the server tells them the bill has already been paid. Can you imagine? What wonderful ways to practice random acts of kindness! These recipients often turn around and do something similar for someone else out of spiritual gratitude for the kindness of a stranger.

Spiritual gratitude is contagious. When we are thankful for something that has happened to us, then we show our appreciation by giving someone else the opportunity to feel spiritual gratitude as well. Random acts of kindness are some of the best ways to create feelings of spiritual gratitude within others. It's also one of the best ways to feel spiritual gratitude at your core by helping others out of the kindness of your heart and simply because you want to do it and not because you're expecting anything in return.

Today make it a point to do one thing for someone else as a random act of kindness. You might open the door for someone, let someone go in front of you in line or help your neighbor paint their house. They'll be surprised and grateful and you'll feel happy because you did something nice for someone who wasn't expecting it.

Exercise: Random Acts of Kindness

Write a list of some of the random acts of kindness that you've experienced. Now pick one and do that same thing for someone else today to pay it forward for others. As you go about your day, look for random acts of kindness from others. Write them down in your journal and you'll have a bigger list to choose from tomorrow.

Discover and Follow Your Divine Path

Just as you discovered your soul purpose; whether it is that of teacher, caregiver, healer or any of the other reasons for your existence, you also have a divine path to follow in order to fulfill this soul purpose. Some people might say your soul purpose and your divine path are the same thing. I believe they are similar but the difference is that your soul purpose is why you're here and your divine path is the route you take and the things you do on your way back home. If, while walking your path you fulfill your purpose, then you've done what you came here to do and learned the lessons you needed to learn while helping others along the way.

Since spiritual gratitude is a core part of our spirit and ingrained within our purpose for being, then practicing gratefulness along the divine path should be automatic. When we are in the spiritual realm, gratitude, love and joy are all shining from us continually but there's something about entering the physical realm that makes it easy to forget these core elements within us. I view the physical realm like a wearing a coat of armor. It's difficult to move, clunky and very protective. When we first arrive we shine in our spirituality. We are a miracle, a gift to the world and our spiritual essence radiates through the eyes of a child. But as we grow, the weight of the world pours down upon us, coating us in a layer of cautionary protection. This in turn pushes the spiritual part of us deeper within our physical being and protects it with walls of armor. As we tune into our soul's purpose and walk our divine path, this layer develops cracks and bit by bit it falls away from us, allowing our frequency to once again shine through as the true spiritual entity that we are.

Each of our divine paths is uniquely our own. It is where we go in life and what we do to fulfill our purpose. For me, my spiritual purpose is that of teacher. I teach on many different levels about many different things. Along my pathway I had to learn to accept the gifts I'd been given before I could teach others how to use them. But my spiritual pathway encompasses a lot more than just teaching metaphysical topics through writing and workshops. I am also a teacher for my children as I, along with my husband, guide them from youth to adulthood. I am a teacher of animals, training them and connecting with them one-on-one. Along my pathway I must experience spiritual gratitude for all that is and try very hard to leave negativity behind. It's not always easy but I do my best and that's all that any one of us can do. My pathway twists and turns, it has carried me to various places, I've known many people in my lifetime and hope to know many more before it's over. I've been blessed with the courage to move forward sharing what I know even in the face of ridicule, I've learned to be thankful because everything is part of my divine path. Spiritual gratitude has taken negativity from me and has opened windows when doors closed. As you walk your own unique divine path, it will do the same for you.

When you're traveling your divine path, you can ensure that negativity doesn't affect you by first being thankful for the challenges negativity presents and by secondly not giving negativity any energy except love and spiritual gratitude. The positive energy of spiritual gratitude and love combined is so strong it completed lights up the darkness of negative energy and it will cause it to move away from you. Your divine path will lead you to peace, joy, satisfaction, gratefulness, love, and happiness in all areas of your life. It will encompass you wholly physically, emotionally, mentally and spirituality. You'll learn more, experience more and become a more complete person overall when you're connected to your soul purpose and following your divine path.

Déjà vu is an indication that you're traveling upon your divine path. It serves as an indicator that you're where you're supposed to be at this moment in time. It can be an indication of things to come because often déjà vu gives you a flash of the future along with the flash of the present moment and it feels like you've experienced it before. This is true because when you planned your current lifetime, you saw the moment of déjà vu.

Another key element of discovering who you really are at a spiritual level and walking your divine path is to understand your Higher Self, your spiritual core essence of the being you are in the spiritual realm. You've taken great steps to learn about your higher self by practicing gratitude as you've progressed through this book. It is also important to know that you can be a teacher—if the student wants to be taught. If you try to force your opinions and beliefs on someone, first that's not acting with spiritual gratitude and secondly they're probably not going to want to hear what you have to say. Walking your own divine path is never an easy task. If it was then you wouldn't learn anything along the way.

Understanding and being grateful for the divinity within you and traveling your divine path will enable you to let go of the past, relish the future and be a beacon of light to those who you meet along the way. You will be empowered, enlightened and become a clearer physical version of the spiritual you within. Do not take your own spirituality to seriously. When you make the journey serious, somber and dull, then you're missing out on the fun, excitement and joy the journey can bring. We each will have an individual experience and none of us walk our divine pathway in the same manner. All you have to do is let your inner light shine.

—10—
How to Activate Thankfulness Now

You can activate your own sense of spiritual gratitude and put it into action in your life to reap its wonderful benefits. When you are gratuitous in spirit it's easy to activate thankfulness in all areas of your life. Taking the time to tune into your own internal sense of spiritual gratitude will help you to experience life in the now. You can teach others to be spiritually grateful too. Lists, boards and charts are excellent tools to use when activating thankfulness. When you know where you've been and where you're going you can remain spiritually grateful at the core of your soul. And when you're grateful within, you can't help but let it shine though you to positively affect those around you. Spiritual gratitude is contagious and a joy to share.

Ready, Set, Activate!

Way back at the beginning of this book you probably made the conscious decision to be more grateful and to live in spiritual gratitude. You've learned about all of the different ways spiritual gratitude can make your life flow in a more positive direction. If you haven't done so already, now is the time to activate your internal sense of spiritual gratitude by making a conscious decision to be more grateful. Once you make your decision, write down the date and time in your spiritual gratitude journal. This gives you a specific starting point to make a positive change in your life and this point can be called your *point of activation.*

As you move forward from your point of activation, know that people who live daily in spiritual gratitude are just like you. They don't have it all going for them, aren't luckier, more unique or any different than you are. What they do have, and what you've been developing through spiritual gratitude, is a keen sense of appreciation for all the bountiful gifts they are given in their lives. They've released feelings of frustration, anger, anxiety, jealousy, hatred, and other negative emotions. They see the blessings all around them and don't take anything or anyone for granted. Being spiritually grateful is all about your perception of the world around you, the people, places and things in your life. It's about connecting to your soul essence on a daily basis and appreciating the gift of your own spiritual self.

For some people activating spiritual gratitude is as simple as deciding to be more thankful and then remembering to do it each day. For others it is easier to write everything down and then review it in order to maintain forward motion. And there are those who plan out what they will be grateful for each day for a week or month in advance so when they look at their agenda, they see a reminder to be thankful. It doesn't matter which method you use, whatever works for you is the best path to follow. You may also start out writing everything down until being spiritually grateful becomes second nature to you and then switch to another method. At that point you may no longer need to write anything down because mindfulness, awareness and thankfulness are now an ingrained part of your being. As you're starting out, use any tools that will help keep you on track. This is where a spiritual gratitude journal comes in handy.

Activating your internal sense of spiritual gratitude also

enables you to become more aware of things like playfulness, affection, laughter, lightheartedness, spontaneity, amusement, and cheerfulness. When you have awareness of these special moments you're able to cherish them even more. You'll feel conscious of every moment as it happens in the here and now, enjoying life to the fullest extent possible. It can change your entire perspective of the world you live in when you are aware of your spiritual self and are thankful for the gifts in your life. It will allow you to live your life to the fullest as the divine being filled with positivity. All you have to do is embrace spiritual gratitude.

The hardest part is deciding to start and sticking with it. If you've ever been on a diet or have watched what you eat, it's a similar process. You have to be aware of what you're doing and you have to care about the end results. When you want to lose weight the end result is a leaner, healthier you. When you activate your internal sense of spiritual gratitude the end result is a more aware and thankful you, which also makes you emotionally healthy. If you don't care about the benefits that you'll receive after your point of activation, then the point of activation becomes a mute point. So before you activate, make sure that you're ready and that you are willing to accept the blessings that you will receive just from being spiritually grateful. If you're not sure, then try on spiritual gratitude for a while before deciding to make it a routine part of your life. I think you'll see such great benefits you'll be ready to activate sooner than you may think. It's all about time. When the time is right for you, on your spiritual path, to allow spiritual gratitude to become a huge part of your life, you'll know it. It will flow freely to you and its integration into your being will be seamless.

Experience Spiritual Gratitude in the Now

Are you in the now of your life? Are you truly present and experiencing each and every moment in full living color? If you're experiencing spiritual gratitude in the now then your life will be vibrant and overflowing with blessings and positive energy. You will feel the significance of the small things in life, the things that you often overlook or take for granted simply because they're always with you. The feel of the sun on your face, a breeze through your hair or love shining from the eyes of someone important to you are just a few of the things you may be overlooking if you're not experiencing spiritual gratitude in the now. If you find that you're not in the now, then you may be going through life skimming the pages of each day instead of being fully involved in your own story. You may face more stumbling blocks than necessary or feel emotionally worn out. You can change your path by focusing on the present, what you're doing at a specific point in time and feeling it with all of your senses, thereby living in the now.

Living in the moment is important once you've made the decision to activate spiritual gratitude in your life. What exactly does living in the moment mean? It's when you're thinking about, where you are, and what you are doing, right now, today. You're not planning for tomorrow, you're not looking back at yesterday but you're living in the moment of now.

Exercise: Living in the Moment

There are a lot of ways that you can begin to live in the moment. Let's do an exercise. I want you to stop reading and look around the area that you're in. Do you see anything (or anyone) that you've taken for granted lately? Look up. Is there a roof over your head or a sunny sky? Maybe you're in your bed, cozy under the covers while you're read. When's the last time you thought about the comfort of a nice mattress? Or the warmth of sheets, blankets or a comforter? Is there running water where you are? Or maybe a lake or fountain? How about birds? Can you hear their song from where you are? What about scents? Do you smell someone's cologne or perfume? Are the neighbors having a barbeque? Does the scent of flowers fill the air? Take a few moments and really pay attention to your surrounding and see if there is anything you have previously taken for granted that you can appreciate by noticing them in the here and now, in this very moment. When you become used to something or accustomed to having someone around it's easy to take it for granted and you don't realize it until you no longer have that thing or person in your life. When you live in the moment you view everything and everyone with fresh eyes each day and appreciate all that is.

Reconnect to Spirit: Reconnecting to your spiritual being helps you live in the moment. When you know who you truly are at a soul level and are reconnected to the divine part of yourself, then positivity surrounds you. You're aware of your own spiritual energy, which makes living in the moment easier than it would be if you weren't connected to your core spiritual essence. It's easier to make deliberate decisions and take specific actions instead of randomly going through life without paying attention.

Triggers: If you find that you're having difficulties implementing spiritual gratitude or that you're still living in the past or worrying about the future, then give yourself a trigger to help you to remember to be thankful. For instance your trigger might be words like *just remember* or *be mindful* or *I'm thankful for*, and then when you're worried or stressed, just think of your trigger words to move yourself back into spiritual gratitude. It may take some time but with practice, you'll soon automatically remember to be give thanks and to live in the moment instead of dwelling on the past or worrying about the future.

Write it down: Another thing you can do is to write down what is worrying you or details of the past event and then after you've written about it, make two columns underneath it. Title the first column "Worrying about this will benefit me because" and title the second column "If I release this I will be". In the first column, write down the benefits that you're receiving from worrying about the event, and in the second column write down what will happen if you let go of the worry. The second column often outweighs the first.

Listen to the Silence: An exercise that I like to do to bring my focus to the now is to listen when it's quiet. Did you know that it isn't really quiet even when it seems that it is? Right now it's quiet in my house as I write this, but if I focus on the now, on everything that I can hear if I really listen carefully, then I hear the keyboard clicking with each letter that I touch, the air conditioner is running, I hear a clock ticking, there is a bird singing outside of my window, the puppies toenails just clicked against the floor when she stretched and I can hear her breathing. A couple of minutes ago I wasn't in the now and wasn't paying particular attention to anything other than what I'm writing, but as I changed my focus and perspective I became aware of all the little things happening around me in this exact moment. Shift your awareness to live in the now of your life.

Teach Others to Be Spiritually Grateful

One of the great things about infusing your life with spiritual gratitude is the ability to share what you've learned with others. When you're able to teach someone else to connect to their spiritual self and to become more aware of the positive effects of thankfulness, it is very fulfilling and enables you to grow on your own spiritual path. Sharing what I've learned over the years about spirituality and spiritual gratitude and the combination of the two together was the purpose behind this book. I thought that if I could share what I've learned with you, then you too could become more aware of the many blessings that you've been given in life.

There are many ways other than writing books that you can do to help other people learn to become spiritually grateful. You are a teacher because you have experienced spiritual gratitude first hand through the reading of this book. I for one am sincerely grateful that you took time from your schedule to spend time with me, reading my words. Feel free to pass along anything that you may have learned here to anyone you encounter in your own life that you feel would benefit from this knowledge. You can also live a giving life by allowing your own sense of spiritual gratitude to shine through in all that you do. Living by example is the best way to teach others how to be grateful. When you spend more time being positive than negative then you're love of life shines forth like a bright light for everyone to see and they will be drawn to your light.

You can also be a shoulder when someone is having a difficult time. Sometimes you can teach another person about spiritual gratitude simply by being there for them when they need you. You might not know exactly what to say depending on the situations, but your presence at that person's side when they need someone you will help them. It's about showing up when you're needed and being a positive influence whenever you can.

Write letters to people you know that express how much they mean to you and how grateful you are to have them in your life. This is again teaching by example but sometimes people need to know that you're thinking about them and appreciate them. You might see them every day but that sticky note that you put on the bathroom mirror that says, "I love and appreciate all that you are and I value you in my life" will make a heart smile. Now you have to mean whatever it is you write on the note, but by sharing your feelings with someone else, you're allowing your spiritual gratitude to shine over them.

Help others learn about their own spirituality. If you're very clear about your own path, or even if you're learning about spirituality, paying it forward by helping others to learn along with you or by teaching what you've learned is a positive way to be grateful for the ability to help others, for the knowledge you've gained, for the students looking for a teacher or a friend to help them along the way. Having faith that everything will work out the way it's supposed to be is another way to show your spiritual gratitude to the divine spirit that you are. It takes faith to believe that everything has a purpose and that life will work out the way it's supposed to, without our forcing issues. Doubt can creep in but spiritual gratitude can help keep it away.

While a lot of people prefer to work on becoming more grateful alone, when you're working with someone else in strengthening your feelings of spiritual gratitude, you help one another stay on track. When one of you falters, the other can bring you back up and help you refocus on the positive. You're teaching each other and are a strong support system for one another. This also works the same way in a group setting with more than two people. Each of you will have different experiences that everyone else can benefit and learn from and that makes adding spiritual gratitude multi-layered and fun.

So take a few minutes right now and think of what you have to offer someone else when it comes to being spiritually grateful. Can you help them develop their spiritual being or can you guide them toward being more thankful for the blessings in their lives? Do you know someone who can benefit from being mindful of spiritual gratitude? If so, why not give them a call and tell them what you're doing and see if it is of interest to them.

Remain Spiritually Grateful at the Core of Your Soul

Knowing yourself is essential to living a balanced life. If you don't know who you are then it's difficult to be firmly rooted in your beliefs. To understand yourself better, think for a moment about how well you know yourself as a spiritual being. What talents, abilities and gifts are uniquely yours? What inspires you at a soul level? What is your life purpose? What is most important to you in this lifetime? What challenges, guides, inspires and motivates you? Are you consciously aware of your actions or do you go through the day speaking and acting without conscious thought of what you're doing and saying? If you are going through your day unaware and just responding out of habit, then it's like living behind a wall of textured glass. You can't see through it clearly. But when you are consciously aware, mindful and spiritually grateful, the wall crumbles away and will leave you with a clear, unobstructed view so that you can consciously make better choices that can transform your life. Keeping a journal along the way will make you an active participant in examining your spiritual nature and the results that spiritual gratitude brings to you.

As you continue on your journey of spiritual gratitude, you will explore a variety of new dimensions within yourself, some of which you may not have known existed before now. You'll be able to see deeper meaning in your life. Knowing who you are, where you've been and where you're going allows you to function with clear intention and thankfulness and to be spiritually grateful at the core of your soul. Using spiritual gratitude with intention will give you results that you will see immediately around you. Actions and reactions will be clearer than ever before. This revelation has to come from deep within you, from the spiritual core of your divine being. While other people can help you along the way and teach you how to make changes so that you can use spiritual gratitude, only you can actually do the internal work required to make the change.

In order to understand how spiritual gratitude and spirituality combine to be a powerful tool for positive forward movement in your life, you first have to be clear about your spiritual beliefs. I'm not talking about a specific religion but instead your beliefs about the soul, the other side, heaven, hell, reincarnation, spiritual purpose, the Universe, angels, spirit guides, intuitive abilities, and so on. To know the nuances of your inner being, you have to know how you feel about each of these ideals and others that your soul feels an attachment to or connection with. It's because these are all part of your spiritual being. Looking at your past and where you've already been in life, will help you to look toward the future and where you want to go. Spiritual gratitude allows you to line your pathway with thankfulness and appreciation, which will allow you to travel this pathway with ease.

Realize that this is a life-long journey. Implementing spiritual gratitude can bring illuminating catalysts that cause you to reflect upon your core inner being and beliefs. You may suddenly realize very specific things about yourself and in accepting and appreciating these moments of recognition you grow and move forward on your spiritual path. Being spiritually grateful can shine a new light on your beliefs. You may find that something you'd always thought of as truth now brings questions to your mind. You may discover that you'd never before considered possible now rings as a Universal truth within your soul. When you appreciate things, more is revealed to you. Such self-realizations can make you think differently about your past because it puts the past into a different perspective.

As you walk this path, live each day with focus, passion and aspiration. Learn from mistakes of the past, think about what you're doing before you do it, while watching what you say because what you put out into the Universe will come back to you. Live an admirable life, one that sets a positive example of spiritual gratitude those around you. Aspire to be more grateful in every aspect of everything that you do. Do not dwell on the flaws within yourself, those around you or situations in which you're involved, but instead look at these imperfections with love and appreciation. In doing so, you may just find perfection. All conditions in your life will affect you according to the attention you give them. If you are positive and thankful, then you'll receive the same in return. If you're negative and ungrateful, then guess what you'll receive? Act with divine grace and you'll be able to handle all that comes your way with joyful spiritual gratitude.

Understanding your past and planning your future also enables to you live in the present. When you're constantly going backward and playing the *what if* or *if only* game within your own mind as you consider the possibilities of what might have happened instead of the reality of what did happen, then you're denying yourself the ability to live in the now or plan the future. Accept the past for what it is: past events that you cannot change no matter how much you wish you could have a different outcome. Appreciate the fact that you were able to have the experience and then release it so that you can create a vacuum for new and wonderful blessings to come your way.

When you know where you're headed in your life, when you understand your soul's purpose and are growing spiritually within yourself, then you are following your divine plan. As spiritual entities we are all connected to divine knowledge and transformative energy through spiritual gratitude, consciousness and the pure essence of our unique spiritual beings. Being spiritually grateful is a way of life for many people. It can be a way of life for you too. You just have to take the first step, set your point of activation and move forward in love, light and spiritual gratitude.

Bibliography

Arrien, Angeles, *Living in Spiritual gratitude: A Journey That Will Change Your Life* Boulder, CO, Sounds True, Inc. 2011.

Beattie, Melody, *Spiritual gratitude: Affirming the Good Things in Life*, Center City, Minnesota, Hazelden Foundation, 2007.

Breathnach, Sarah Ban, *The Simple Abundance Companion: Following Your Authentic Path to Something More*, New York, New York, Warner Books, Inc. 2000.

Demoss, Nancy Leigh, *Choosing Spiritual gratitude: Your Journey to Joy*, Chicago, IL, Moody Publishers, 2009.

Hay, Louise L., *Spiritual gratitude A Way of Life*, Carlsbad, California, The Hay Foundation, 1996.

Kralik, John, *A Simple Act of Spiritual gratitude: How Learning to Say Thank You Changed My Life*, New York, New York, Hyperion, 2010.

Lesowitz, Nina and Sammons, Mary Beth, Living Life as a Thank You: The Transformative Power of Daily Spiritual gratitude, San Francisco, CA, Viva Editions, 2009.

Prochaska, James O., Norcross, John, and DiClemente, Carlo, *Changing for Good: A Revolutionary Six-Stage Program for Overcoming Bad Habits and Moving Your Life Positively Forward*, New York, New York, William Morrow and Company/Avon

Books. 1994.

Webster's New World™ Dictionary and Thesaurus, Second Edition, New York, New York, Hungry Minds, Inc. 2002.

Young, Janet, *The Subconscious Mind and its Illuminating Light, An Interpretation*, San Francisco, California, 1909.

Photo by Isabel Barney

Melissa Alvarez is a multi-published, award-winning author. She writes nonfiction under her real name and paranormal romantic suspense as Ariana Dupré. She owns Friesian horses, Barock Pinto horses and German Shepherd dogs with her husband and together they are successful breeders of champions. She enjoys reading, spending time with her family and horses, and designing book covers when she's not writing. Melissa lives in sunny South Florida. Visit her online at MelissaA.com for updates on new releases or at BookCovers.Us or BookCoversGalore.com if you're an author in need of a cover designer.

www.ingramcontent.com/pod-product-compliance
Lightning Source LLC
Chambersburg PA
CBHW060515100426
42743CB00009B/1327